MEMOIR *of the*
HAWK

MEMOIR *of the* HAWK

poems

James Tate

An Imprint of HarperCollinsPublishers

HarperCollins books may be purchased for educational, business, or sales promotional use. For information please write: Special Markets Department, HarperCollins Publishers Inc., 10 East 53rd Street, New York, NY 10022.

First Ecco paperback edition published 2002

Designed by Cassandra J. Pappas

The Library of Congress has catalogued the hardcover edition as follows:

Tate, James.
    Memoir of the hawk : poems / by James Tate.—1st ed.
      p. cm.
    ISBN 0-06-621017-8 (hardcover)
    I. Title.

PS3570.A8 M46 2001
811'.54—dc21   00-067696

ISBN 0-06-093543-x (pbk.)

02 03 04 05 06 BG/QM 10 9 8 7 6 5 4 3 2 1

For Dara

Contents

Acknowledgments

American Poetry Review, The Best of the Prose Poem, Boulevard, Conduit, Conjunctions, Denver Quarterly, Fence, Gettysburg Review, Harvard Review, Lit, Massachusetts Review, New Republic, Ontario Review, Poetry, Poetry International, Prose Poem International, Southern California Anthology, Volt, Washington Square Review

"Then I went back into the house and wrote, It is midnight. The rain is beating on the windows. It was not midnight. It was not raining."

—Samuel Beckett,
Molloy

NEW BLOOD

A huge lizard was discovered drinking
out of the fountain today. It was not menacing
anyone, it was just very thirsty. A small crowd
gathered and whispered to one another, as though
the lizard would understand them if they spoke
in normal voices. The lizard seemed not even
a little perturbed by their gathering. It drank
and drank, its long forked tongue was like a red
river hypnotizing the people, keeping them in a
trance-like state. "It's like a different town,"
one of them whispered. "Change is good," the
other one whispered back.

VALE OF THE WHITE HORSE

That's where I first met my bride. She
was standing under a chestnut tree during a
summer shower. I stopped my car and offered
to give her a lift. She didn't seem to hear me.
I got out of the car and walked up to her.
Her skin looked and felt like porcelain. "Are
you okay?" I asked. She blinked her eyes as if
coming out of a trance. "I was looking for
the white horse," she said. I drove her to
a hospital where the doctor diagnosed her as
being my bride. "There's no doubt about it,
she is your bride." We kissed, and thus the Trans-
Canadian Highway was born.

I MUST HAVE BEEN THAT MAN

Over at Archie's Soda & Sandwich Shop
he ordered the bacon, lettuce and tomato
and then laughed out loud, appeared
as one with a past now officially over
and headed for a ballgame or something
that won't wrench a soul too far
out of shape. We watched him for a while
just because of that one laugh, and then
he started to stare at us, not aggressively,
but as if he wanted to be asked over.
Finally, I went up to him and invited him
to our table. "Do I look that lonely?"
he asked. "Well, maybe I am and maybe I'm not,
but I accept your hospitality either way."
He wasn't stingy with his words,
but sometimes they were hard to follow.
He'd had a parachute accident in the military
and had been hospitalized for several years.
They had taken good care of him, but now
he had very little memory of anything before.
He wasn't unhappy, he said, just curious.
No one, as far as he knew, visited him
in all his time in the hospital.
Several of us could barely hold back our tears.
"Of course there was a nurse," he said,
"there's always a nurse, right? Gena,
Gena would bathe me when I didn't need bathing,
she was one bathin' nurse. She should've
gotten the Nobel Prize for bathing."
"Did you love her?" Barbara asked.
"I don't suppose it's a good idea
to love someone just because they pity you,
but if you can't help yourself there's
worse things than being a fool."
We sat in silence awhile. Finally, I said,

"Mind if I ask what you were laughing about
up there at the counter by yourself?"
"Well, the bad news is there never was a Gena.
But the good news is there wasn't a fall
from a parachute either. So see how
it all works out. Nice, isn't it, nice and easy."
With that he got up and walked away.
Later, Barbara said, "He wasn't lying
about Gena, he did love her. I know he did."
"But what about the fall?" I said.
"I suspect there was some kind of fall," she said,
"even if it was just a little stumble."

TE DEUM LAUDAMUS

A plover shot up from under a bush and
scared me. I had been watching a pilot perform
stunts overhead, free-falling, turning over and
over, which already had me dizzy and the sudden
noise and appearance of the plover nearly knocked
me over, delicate thing that I am. I gave up
watching the pilot and walked as quickly as I
could toward town. A woman with a thorn in her
forehead sat on the steps of Town Hall. She was
feeding breadcrumbs to a flock of pigeons. A
bead of blood around the thorn, blue sky, people
scurrying to pay their water bills, parking tickets.

YOUNG MAN WITH A HAM

I'm watching him from my window. He's clutching
the ham as if it were a football everyone wants
to steal. He keeps looking over his shoulder and
stopping to make sure the ham is secure in his grip.
No one's on the street but him. But wait, old Mr. Wilson,
who lives down the street from me, has suddenly
appeared in his fedora and suspenders and is jogging
as best he can after the young man. I go out onto
the porch to watch. The young man has not yet seen
Mr. Wilson. Then in the last minute he spots him
and starts to run. To my great amazement, Mr. Wilson
dives through the air and tackles him. They wrestle
and grunt. Mr. Wilson wrenches the ham free, gets
away and starts racing down the street with the ham.
Clearly it's his ham now.

THE LOVELY ARC OF A METEOR
IN THE NIGHT SKY

At the party there were those sage souls
who swam along the bottom like those huge white
fish who live for hundreds of years but have no
fun. They are nearly blind and need the cold.
William was a stingray guarding his cave. Only
those prepared for mortal battle came close to
him. Closer to the surface the smaller fish
played, swimming in mixed patterns only a god
could decipher. They gossiped and fed and sparred
and consumed, and some no doubt even spawned.
It's a life filled with agitation, thrills,
melodrama and twittery, but too soon it's over.
And nothing's revealed because it was never known.

A TRUE STORY

I was on my lunch break, sitting on a bench
in the park, when a cute little doggy came up to
me and said, "Excuse me, sir, I'm sorry to disturb
you like this, but would you permit me to have a bite
of your sandwich? I am not a beggar by inclination,
but circumstances beyond my control have withered
my pride. I am lost and confused. My owner seems
to have abandoned me, and I have had nothing to
eat for six days."

"Dear friend," I said, "please take what is
left of this sandwich. I must return to work, but
if you would meet me here at five o'clock, I would
happily take you with me to my home. And, with
your approval, I would gladly keep you and feed
you every day. I think you would be happy there,
and I'm sure you would bring me much joy."

The dog agreed to meet him at the bench, but
when the man returned there was a note on the bench.
Written in perfect schoolboy script, it read:
"Sir, it is with a sense of shame that I must decline
your generous offer. For the past six days I have
perpetrated the same scam on you, and you have
generously given me your lunch, for which I am
grateful. However, your lack of memory worries me
and how it would affect my existence in your household. With all due respect, sir, living by one's
wits in the park suits me just fine."

CUNNING

I had gotten a nasty bite at the petting
zoo earlier that day. On the bus home I sat
next to a little old lady, tiny and stooped,
her head bobbing up and down. I don't know why
I did this, but I showed her the bite on my hand.
She stared at it for a long time. Then she
reached out and took my hand in her papery
blue-veined hands. She brought my hand closer
to her eyes. Her mouth was open just a little
and my heart started to race. I jerked my
hand out of her grip just in time. She smiled
and showed me her teeth. "They're beautiful,"
I said. "Brand-new," she replied.

THE LITTLE BROTHER

Back then the streets were made of goose down.
The ice-cream man rang his bell and threw bricks
at the little children, who in turn set his truck
on fire. Yes, I remember every little blade of grass
I ever set foot on, and the flowers, the flowers
I would have sold my mother's life for. . . .

Grandmother's cooking could have killed us all,
but it didn't. We grew strong and massive
butting and swatting one another at the table
over rights to the last slab of charred meat.
Father and mother cackled and howled at our ferocity.
And grandmother was flattered that we so adored her dainties.

Summer nights we'd roam the streets, hungry for love
or something gooey and strange. The girls couldn't stay away from
us, or if they could, we'd catch them and make them
listen to our jokes and feel our muscles.
It was a harmless game and I, for one, never got
anywhere with them, except lonelier and more depressed.

My brothers were such liars I never believed a word
they said. They all had been in jail for spitting on cops.
Now if that isn't stupid! But when they left home
before me I cried each time. And all these years later
I don't know where even one of them lives, not one letter
or phone call. Still, no one can take my memories,

and who would want them, anyway, my souvenirs?

YOU DON'T KNOW ME

Sometimes you hear a xylophone
deep in the forest and you know
that things are just not right.
Vichyssoise beneath a canopy
with several unnamable beautiful
peekaboos may have gotten me off
to a less than promising start,
so a chickadee gyrating in my ear
and a catbird spilled the champagne
and a dog waygone chainsawed
some pleasure I left on the table
for a tip, an itsy-bitsy gratuity.
I got home on the back of a grackle,
poky me. In the big chair I started
whistling and singing a melody:
It was the forest tune, about bugs
and sunlight and snakes and mumbo jumbo.
And now it is your turn to burn,
the song said, but first you must travel
to Cameroon unapprehended
in the eye of a cold, dead hurricane.
You're starting to annoy me, I said.
I was trying to annoy you, the song said,
to see if you were really listening.
There's a hole in my head, I said,
I was hoping you would help to fill.
What do you take me for, skillet biscuits?
Perhaps. But you are also the forest song
which is long and deep and clear.
I exist but I have no purpose, the song said,
but I'll pour some cool water over you
that you will not soon forget.

"Did you ever meet Old Anthony Now-Now?"

"Yes, I'm proud to say I did have the good fortune
to meet Old Anthony Now-Now. Even in his dotage he could
sew a button on a jet plane."

"And he was a wonderful kisser. One night at a party
he asked me what was the most times I had ever been kissed.
I told him the Father of French Surgery had once kissed me
two hundred and seventy-six times in an evening, and Old
Anthony, after asking my approval, proceeded to kiss me
two hundred and seventy-five times, stopping, he said,
so as not to be disrespectful. Fine kisses they were, too."

"The Little Man of Twickenham kissed me for seven hours
straight once and we barely took a breath in all that time.
They were once in a lifetime kisses I'll never forget."

"Did I mention The Discrowned Glutton?"

"Not today."

"Now, there was a poor kisser."

"I think we'd both agree that nobody can compare with
The Illustrious Conqueror of Common Sense. He only kissed
me once but it was as if a bird of paradise shot through
my whole body and I woke more alive than I've ever been."

"Oh yes, even better than the Bee-Lipped Oracle!"

THE STORM AND STRESS PERIOD

I wandered the city peering into shop windows
as if for a clue. If a mannequin seemed to be
pointing in a certain direction I would go there
and then check another window. A doll was sleeping
in a cradle, so I curled up on a park bench and
took a nap. In my dream I was feeding peanuts
to a rat. It was standing on its haunches
looking completely happy. A siren of some sort
woke me. I straightened my tie and went to work
at Sparky's Life Insurance, where I am their True
Blue Knight of the Rueful Countenance, and my sole
job is to feed some peanuts to the company rat
every now and then.

ENDLESS TIME

The donkey stood alone in the paddock
swishing its tail to rid itself of flies.
It was a hot day, but billowing white clouds
occasionally blocked out the sun's rays.
The donkey shook its head and wiggled its
ears, blinked its eyes and now and then
kicked its legs. At night, when no one is
around, it leaps over the barns and turns
somersaults in the air. It is a way of
relieving tension, the donkey's mother
explains to the farmer's wife.

SLOW DAY AT MANNY'S

Appliances were on our minds all morning.
We tried changing subjects: "That holy war
is a real doozy, isn't she?" Or:
"How's your mother doing? I'm sorry I asked."
Nothing worked. Every attempt ended biliously.
So I finally suggested that we go on down
to Manny's, not to buy anything, but just
to hang out for a while, mingle with the merchandise.
And it felt good, it was a relief to touch
the newfangled, glass-topped stoves, the automatic
ice-making refrigerators, the huge wide-screened
TVs. The two salesmen tried out some small talk
with us, and we politely asked a few relevant
questions. I started watching a game show playing
on about fifteen televisions simultaneously.
I thought, so this must be how a fly sees,
and I was feeling very fly-like and I liked it.
I didn't want to stop being a fly, I was just
pausing in my fly-life to watch this human
game show because I apparently had nothing
more pressing to do just then and I wanted
to know how they lived and what they lived for.
I was glad I was a fly until Josie tapped me
on my head and I looked around and she had
a blender under her arm and I flew around the room
several time buzzing my little brains out.
It was a slow day at Manny's until we got there.
One of the salesmen was named Doctor Ecstaticus
and he was a famous mystic who just happened
to believe in the healing power of appliances.

THE WORKFORCE

Do you have adequate oxen for the job?
No, my oxen are inadequate.
Well, how many oxen would it take to do an adequate job?
I would need ten more oxen to do the job adequately.
I'll see if I can get them for you.
I'd be obliged if you could do that for me.
Certainly. And do you have sufficient fishcakes for the men?
We have fifty fishcakes, which is less than sufficient.
I'll have them delivered on the morrow.
Do you need maps of the mountains and the underworld?
We have maps of the mountains but we lack maps of the underworld.
Of course you lack maps of the underworld,
there are no maps of the underworld.
And, besides, you don't want to go there, it's stuffy.
I had no intention of going there, or anywhere for that matter.
It's just that you asked me if I needed maps. . . .
Yes, yes, it's my fault, I got carried away.
What do you need, then, you tell me?
We need seeds, we need plows, we need scythes, chickens,
pigs, cows, buckets and women.
Women?
We have no women.
You're a sorry lot, then.
We are a sorry lot, sir.
Well, I can't get you women.
I assumed as much, sir.
What are you going to do without women, then?
We will suffer, sir. And then we'll die out one by one.
Can any of you sing?
Yes, sir, we have many fine singers among us.
Order them to begin singing immediately.
Either women will find you this way or you will die
comforted. Meanwhile busy yourselves
with the meaningful tasks you have set for yourselves.
Sir, we will not rest until the babes arrive.

FAMILY SORROW

I was alone in the house reading the evening
paper and sipping a glass of sherry when a note
arrived by courier informing me that my brother
had been hospitalized. He had fallen from his
horse and was paralyzed. This struck me as funny
on two accounts: 1. I have no brother, and 2.
he has no horse. Nonetheless, I changed into my
tragic suit and quickly caught a taxi. At the
hospital "my brother" looked awful, but was exceed-
ingly happy to see me. I kissed him on the brow
and struggled to hold back tears. After a brief
chat, the nurse came in and injected him with something that made him turn green. "For the pain,"
she assured me. He began to smell like Walt
Whitman, so I crawled home, pausing only to sniff
at passing dogs and policemen.

WITCHES

There are all kinds of druids and
witches living in the hills around here.
They don't hurt anybody as far as we know.
But you can always spot them at the grocery
store. First off, they drive these really
broken-down old pickup trucks, often with
handmade wooden shelters over beds
like they could live in there. And they're
covered in layers of shawls and scarves
and bedecked with long gaudy earrings
and necklaces and bracelets. And always
the long, long hair. They buy huge amounts
of supplies, twenty pounds of cheese, giant
bags of granola, etc. They move quickly
as if afraid of being burned at a stake.
We all know who they are and like having
them among us on their secret missions
to decorate their inner Christmas trees
with bedeviled human chickenbones.

SUDDEN INTEREST IN THE DEAD

Never once in all those years did Jack
visit his mother in the madhouse. After he
was a grown man and his mother was still confined
there was nothing to stop him from visiting her,
but he did not. It left a black hole in him
that nothing could fill. He traveled, he drank
too much, he loved, he painted and wrote, but
he would not visit his poor, insane mother.
When he was at last notified of her death, he
didn't shed a tear. He began to shake and shudder
and was soon carried off by wild beasts.

THE EXPERIMENT WITH JOHN

Sue and I knew that Marcy was an alien,
but John, her husband, did not, or at least
he didn't let on if he did know. Her eyes
were a dead giveaway, oblong and stuck in
at a slant, but worse than that was her smile.
She smiled at the most inappropriate times,
such as when she told of John losing his job,
or John having to give up his beloved antique
car or John falling ill. All this was cause
for beaming as Marcy told it. She wasn't cruel,
she simply lacked a human heart. Where she came
from human pain was funny. And that's why
they sent her here, to laugh at us and make
us feel worse. Sue and I would like to make
her feel pain, to know what it's like, but we
know it's impossible. She's way too metallic.

AN AFTERNOON IN HELL

He cries awhile, for no apparent reason.
Sniffs, blows his nose. Then goes about his
business, stomp, pound, smash, crush, explode.
Then cries a little more, sob, blubber, bleat.
It's awful, he says. It's of no use. He throws
his chair through the window. It's a mess, he says.
The whole damned thing is useless. Now he's
really weeping, cascades, waterfalls, rivers.
I shouldn't bother, he says. It's a big, miserable
waste of time. His wife walks in. Honey,
haven't you finished changing the baby yet?
   Almost finished, he chirps.

MEMORY

A little bookstore used to call to me.
Eagerly I would go to it
hungry for the news
and the sure friendship.
It never failed to provide me
with whatever I needed.
Bookstore with a donkey in its heart,
bookstore full of clouds and
sometimes lightning, showers.
Books just in from Australia,
books by madmen and giants.
Toucans would alight on my stovepipe hat
and solve mysteries with a few chosen words.
Picasso would appear in a kimono
requesting a discount, and then
laugh at his own joke.
Little bookstore with its belly
full of wisdom and confetti,
with eyebrows of wildflowers—
and customers from Denmark and Japan,
New York and California, psychics
and lawyers, clergymen and hitchhikers,
the wan, the strong, the crazy,
all needing books, needing directions,
needing a friend, or a place to sit down.
But then one day the shelves began to empty
and a hush fell over the store.
No new books arrived.
When the dying was done,
only a fragile, tattered thing remained,
and I haven't the heart to name it.

MENTAL-HEALTH WORKERS

Mostly we were able to ignore the hairy thing
in the corner. It seemed to be leaking some green
fluid, but we could walk around that. It gave off
an unpleasant odor, a cross between Limburger cheese
and a decomposing skunk, but we never mentioned it.
We didn't seem to have a plan for getting rid of it.
It wasn't really hurting anybody. And then one day
I thought I heard it singing. And another day it
seemed to say I love you. And then one day it wasn't
there anymore, not lost but gone before.

SEPTEMBER

Near September the moose retreat to the
ice-cream shops. A flotilla of hunters sinks
to the bottom of the lake singing "Pennies from
Heaven." A little girl in green pajamas is
swinging from a maple tree. The maple tree
is blushing but still manages to whisper its
love for her. September is coming, balancing
a thousand-and-one gifts on its head and
shoulders, twittering as if someone were
tickling it. "It's coming," shouts the woodsman.
A priest was prattling on about his disappoint-
ments in love until two white doves flew
out of his eyes and drew a thunderous applause
from everyone.

THE SECOND MRS. TYLER

She woke covered in emerald dreams. They
drank their tea in a wavering mist, and then
dressed in fallen leaves. All this in a silence
with its mouth half open. The day rolled by
in a little wagon made of gold. By noon she
was ready for bed again. They swam to an island
made of butterflies and loved while the wind
sang a song about fire and the soul and long
journeys with no end and no beginning. They voted
for a giraffe to represent them and were arrested
and fell asleep again.

BEHIND THE MILK BOTTLE

is a crust of bread and three dead ladybugs,
also a flashlight and some Band-Aids.
In case of a power outage I'm all set.
Rubbing two dead ladybugs together
creates a bluish green light
by which one can enjoy the crust of bread
and forget about the hurricane or whatever.
I keep an extra in case one explodes.
Once as a river of molten lava
poured through my living room
I was cut off from my emergency kit,
my Band-Aids and so on, and had to crawl
out the window and go around.
The kitchen floor was like a frying pan,
so I sprung through the air and grabbed
my stuff and then went back around
and crawled back into the living room window,
though in this case it turned out
I never employed the items in my kit
as the lava ceased in less than a week.
As for pillagers, think twice:
behind the milk bottle is another milk bottle
and a nest of unruly ribbons
and a ghost who barks at airplanes.

THINKING AHEAD TO POSSIBLE OPTIONS
AND A WORST-CASE SCENARIO

I swerved to avoid hitting a squirrel
in the center of the road and that's when
the deer came charging out of the forest
and forced me to hit the brakes for all I
was worth and I careened back to the other
side of the road just as a skunk came toddling
out of Mrs. Bancroft's front yard and I swung
back perhaps just grazing it a bit. I glanced
quickly in the rearview mirror and in that
instant a groundhog waddled from the side
of the road and I zigzagged madly and don't
know if I nipped it or not because up ahead I
could see a coyote stalking the Colliers'
cat. Oh well, I said, and drove the rest
of the way home without incident.

T.B. BLUES

The step is a step Keats himself
jumped over.

The step is a step Keats himself
dropped his glove on.

The step is a step Keats himself
died for.

The step is a step Keats himself
avoided.

The step is a step Keats himself
peed on.

The step is a step Keats himself
made whoopee on.

The step is a step Keats himself
burned the letters of the alphabet on.

The step is a step Keats himself
never took.

The step is a step Keats himself
sat on for two hours or more

whistling a tune Jimmie Rodgers
would write 100 yrs. down the line.

BOOM-BOOM

A man and a woman meet in all alley. They kiss
but they don't really know one another. You smell
like violets, he says putting his hand on her breast.
You're strong, she says rubbing herself on his thigh.
He runs his hands through her hair and pulls her tighter
to him. I must have you, he says. Yes, I want to
make love to you, she says touching him between his
legs. Yes, you must give up your treasure to fructify the crops, he says. Oh yes, I want to fructify
very much, she says. The crops, I mean.

GRAND OPERA

Looky here, these little children
we called our friends, they've had
their lives now. Irma was a beauty
but married badly—I could have told her
that. And Jack, Jack was tough and thought
war was a walk in the woods, and he
never came back. And towheaded Tommy
stares at a stucco wall in Florida
with bats in his belfry. The possibilities
of life are limitless, and most often
so surprising—the dolt becomes
the genius and vice versa, the old
vice versa principle working overtime
to keep us interested, or at least
confused. All truly wise men claim
to know nothing. Spend your days
divesting (give it all to me, I'm
collecting!). Marjorie of the pigtails
and gap teeth ran off with a petty gangster
and I'm told they've done quite well.
And Paul the cheapskate who could fix
anything ended his life as a radical
martyr for a cause I never even understood.
Out of nothing something clings to me.
It's my little kit bag that I love,
that and the wind, always about to start
my masterpiece, although my head is splitting, my feet hurt.
It is often said that we operate in a vacuum,
but who is we?
Great is the day with its potato nestled in the dark.

MADONNA OF THE CHAIR

She had many hobbies. She collected
stamps, coins, dolls, and autographs of
famous people. Not many people know this
about her, but she was an expert jai alai
player. For a brief time she owned and ran
a cosmetics company, but after the birth of
her son she wanted to stay home and play
with her wild goat. Her husband worried
that she might like the goat better than
him, so he gave her a chair.

HOW THE PEOPLE ARE GOVERNED

Even empty-handed, Toby looked as if he was
about to chop something down. His friends
thought he had probably killed at least one
person sometime or other. And what's strange
about all this is that he was one heck of a nice
guy. I liked him, and I figured he might kill
me at any moment. Why was this? His smile
was infectious, but it did feel like it was
dripping blood. Then one day he and his mother
moved to a small town in Iowa, where they opened
a flower shop called Murder, Inc. and by all
accounts it is very successful. Many of us
are still a little frightened and miss him
more each passing day.

INTROSPECTION

I look inward and I see a desert with some
tall cacti and a few snakes lying around waiting
for a careless mouse, and in back of that there
is a range of snow-crested mountains, and a lynx
and a brown bear are drinking from a clear pool
of water, and down below on the other side is a
village going about its business. Mrs. Harvey
has just made her deposit in the Farmers' Bank,
and Elijah Williams has purchased several packets
of seeds at the hardware store. That's all I can
see at the moment. Wait, Jemima Williams is just now
stepping out of her bathtub!

AN AFTERNOON STROLL

You don't know if you are being followed,
so you dip into a department store,
and, disguising yourself as a shopper,
you buy several expensive items.
On the next street corner you stop a policeman
and ask him, "Are you also a Nature poet?"
He smiles and nods yes indeed he is.
You invite him to join your secret club
and he is delighted. "See you Saturday!"
A day which started off rather dismally
turns a sharp right and there up ahead
is the prospect of something sweet with
an officer of the law, who is now following you.
So you slip into the cigar store,
and, though you have never been a smoker,
you stock up on some very fine stogies.
Miles on a bench beckoned me and I sat
half-expecting paradise to attack.
A pigeon blinked at my feet, and my head
spun around in search of a tail.
No one conspicuous was on my case,
or maybe I'm just losing my edge.
I sat there blowing smoke into
the wee hunger of nothing's eye.
My pajamas were as blue as the ocean,
and choppy, too. They were very choppy.

TRAVELER

She stood between the door and the chair,
her head hung in preternatural sadness, as if
she had been there always. I walked around her
several times, but she took no notice of me.
I had wanted to share the sunset with her and
perhaps have a drink on the terrace, a few
moments of intimacy. She might tell me again
of her childhood in Tibet, her favorite tiger.
Instead, she has gone there by herself to watch
her mother die, holding her hand. Poor child
alone in all the universe, without sunsets,
without even me.

BLANC IS NOIR

I cannot really see these things,
the drosophila leisurely teasing me.
I'm not quite oriented, rickracking
from one store to another, bought this
instead of that, hello unnamed person,
weaving in and out, nausea, mistrust,
yes, I want that one, I mean that one,
then preening in the mirror, game theory,
gaping, galvanized, galvanic skin response,
don't forget to breathe—it seems obvious
but you'd be surprised how many—trying
to navigate, to find my way back,
the this and the that, the drivers
barely able to steer and shouting
something unintelligible, squeegeeing
like squint modifiers in a sentence,
we're all diplopic. But once home
I think I got more for my money
and am pleased as punch with myself,
fall down on the sofa, swat the cat,
drift into a coma where strange appliances
tell me I'm an excellent human being.

WAR AND PEACE

Someone has hit me on the head with a book
and I'm falling down. Okay, now I'm down. I
close my eyes. An ostrich is charging me. She
seems furious. I open my eyes. An ostrich is
hurtling toward me. I close my eyes. I'm on
the green bank of a babbling brook. My beloved
is beside me. It would be indelicate of me to
say more. But we did have a grass sandwich
after sundown.

OUR LADY OF THE SHIVERS

We would dance in the moonlight under
her steady gaze. Dancing led to smooching
and since she didn't approve of this or anything we did we didn't stop ourselves from
full enjoyment. The stony bitch invoked
the cruelest winds to deprive us of our
pleasure. It didn't work. Her piety in-
flamed our passion and she melted into a
little puddle of skimble-skamble moonshine.
The blue devils swimming in it were pleasing
to the eye.

HOTEL OF THE GOLDEN DAWN

It was clear to us that the real owners
of the hotel were spiders. They were everywhere
but you had to look carefully. They had ingenious
ways of disguising themselves, except for the
clerk at the check-in desk. He was clearly a
spider, a pale pink translucent spider, a kindly
one. In fact, in my experience, all the spiders
in the hotel were benevolent. One stroked my
brow as I lay in bed trying to sleep. Another
kept flies off of my eggs in the morning. Many
of the guests I saw in the lobby seemed to me
inhuman, or at least toothless and drained of
their blood. It was a convention of some kind,
button makers, astronomers, comedians, florists,
prison guards, lamplighters, editors, whatever,
and they were having a very good time. The desk-
spider and the door-spider eyed them proudly.

YEAR OF PROGRESS

After the storm had passed we went
outside to assess the damage. A large
branch had been broken off the willow and
the tulips had had their brains beaten out
by the hail. The lawn boy statue had toppled
and the hand holding the lantern was cracked
but holding on. All the seed had been blown
from the bird feeders. And as we walked the
sun was coming out, the sky was blue. Two
old men stood in the middle of the road
arguing over a pair of dentures that had
been snitched by the wind.

MAINE

Driving north at sunset, we were sure we'd
see a moose. All the conditions were right: swampy
woodlands on both sides of the road, lakes nearby,
and the road was affectionately nicknamed "Moose
Alley." How could we not see a moose? We drove
slowly and stopped when circumstances virtually
demanded it, moose-shaped shadows grazing between
vine-draped trees. Anything could be a moose.
Nearly everything was. Several times we turned off
the road onto rough dirt roads and drove slowly
until we came to wooden bridges above the rippling
stream banked by rushes and we were sure we would
see at least one. Then darkness fell like a
moose upon us. Giant moose shades guided us back
out of the wilderness and we were much obliged.

PRECIOUS LITTLE WE CAN DO

The clubhouse was bedecked with blue ribbons
perhaps symbolizing the simpler days of water
splashing everywhere. We were just out for a drive
when we saw it and thought it must mean something
or the boys were having a party tonight because
one of them just turned seventy and was feeling
kind of blue. The older they get the friskier
they get, that's the rule around here anyway.
We drove down to the pond just to see some water
and then the ducks came over and we talked to them
for an hour or so, mostly about things they
couldn't understand. I think that's why
they stayed and talked back so vociferously.
It was cloudy and then it was sunny and then
a big car drove up and some newlyweds got out
and started singing. The ducks were frightened
and frankly so were we, and our fear brought us
closer. We waddled toward the water prestissimo
and paddled for the cattails and water lilies
on the far side, our panic given way to serenity.
The couple left at the end of the song.
A great blue heron circled overhead. We climbed
ashore and shook off what water we could, and feathers.
We wrapped ourselves in some blanket from the trunk.
On the way home, my wife, who can be very cruel
when she wants to be, says to me, "I prefer
the company of loons, their insane, crazy laughter
is a comfort for which there is no substitute."
Later that night, I joined the boys at the clubhouse.
They signed in unison and repeated, "There is precious
little we can do, precious little we can do."

TOADS TALKING BY A RIVER

A book can move from room to room
without anyone touching it. It can climb
the staircase and hide under the bed. It
can crawl into bed with you because it knows
you need company. And it can read to you
in your sleep and you wake a smarter person
or a sadder person. It is good to live
surrounded by books because you never know
what can happen next: lost in the inter-
stellar space between teacups in the cupboard,
found in the beak of a downy woodpecker,
the lovers staring into the void and then
jumping over it, flying into their beautiful
tomorrows like the heroes of a storm.

WHEREABOUTS

We dug that tunnel with spoons. We
wanted to know what was on the other side
and we didn't know how else to get there.
Years went by, men died, children grew old.
It was our way of life, our tunneling life.
"Will you be tunneling with us tomorrow, John?"
"Of course I'll be tunneling with you tomorrow,
Jim, what else do you think I'd be doing?"
People from other towns came to tunnel with
us as well. They brought their own spoons
and tunneled with the same vigor.
    When daylight first shone through on the
other side we jumped back like frightened rats.
A ragamuffin poked her face into the light
and said, "If you're looking for New York City,
it's the other way."

MY PRIVATE TASMANIA

has never been discovered,
is thought to be the source of all fire,
is a pigpen for the soul,
changes its shape and location
when you try to think of it.
It smells like a funeral parlor
full or orchids and makes you
want to run for your life.
And at the same time it's sexual,
salacious, creating a terrible hunger.
My Tasmania conceals beneath her
raven-black apron hundreds of
unknown species of wild pigs.
It rocks in the wind at night
and hums a beautiful melody.
Even the birds can't sleep
and begin to sing extinct songs.
Snakes are counting their worry beads.
I'm walking in circles,
getting closer and closer.
Walls of the coal mine
that is my head
begin to cave in, crashing
in huge chunks to the floor,
shocking the bats out of their dreams
and the rats out of gnawing
on one another. Closer, I said,
I must be getting closer.
The smell of rotting flesh
was gagging me. I couldn't see
through the smoke and haze.
I stop circling, begin to laugh.
My mother says, "Jimmy, please
stop laughing, you're frightening us."

AT THE END OF THE LITTLE STREET

Chugging along on a wing and a prayer,
I stopped at the candy store and gave old
Mrs. Harrington her birthday present—a fifth
of bourbon. She kissed me a little more
enthusiastically than I wanted, but I do
know how she loves her bourbon. She smokes
those little cigarillos all day long and that
leaves the shop smelling worse than a glue
factory, but she's good to all the neighborhood kids and that's what matters. I peeled
her off my chest, said a hasty goodbye
and escaped out into the street. I took
a quick nip from my flask and reflected on
Mrs. Harrington's long smoky kiss. By God,
once she's kissed you, you stay kissed!

OVERCOMING SELF-CONSCIOUSNESS

The hounds of hell were at my ankles,
and then they passed me and were at her
ankles, and then they passed her and she
looked extraordinarily relieved and collapsed
into my arms and we fell in love and now
we often reminisce about our days of peril
and can even laugh about the fear we had
felt and how we had imagined the worst
that could have happened torn limb from
limb by the fury in those dogs, those small
hairless shadows now drowned in the River
of Paradise.

REMEMBERABILITY

A scarlet tanager shot low overhead,
its singular bright color shocked us,
a smudge of lipstick in a great hurry.
We were fresh off the ferry walking
in the Battery after the Statue of Liberty.
We can't hide our love.
And New York is forever new to us.
If we could sing we would, but we can't.
So we talk freely, endlessly,
full of ideas and opinions.
And I remember the zebra that paused
to compliment you on your hair,
just what she had always dreamed of, she said.
"My hair for your coat," you said.
The zebra slowly looked back at its torso,
and then back at you with sadness
and longing in her eyes.
Then we all had a good laugh.
"That's why I love this city," she said,
"everyone's a comedian."

PLENTITUDE

A thunderstorm has passed.
I sit on the front stoop reading a novel
about a man who thinks man's whole purpose
is to destroy one another and the planet.
He doesn't strike me as a bad man.
The novel is written in a felicitous manner
and it is highly intelligent.
So the darkness is rich and loamy
and it feels cool and healthy
to run your hands through it.
An aristocrat and successful businessman
(two more attributes he disdains in himself),
he doesn't believe in love or lovemaking,
but admits that he is addicted to both.
I'm glad I'm not like this man,
though an evening spent in his company
would not repel me. More likely
I'd feel pity, but not of the condescending kind.
It's like dying before your life is over,
a breathing, walking dead man.
"Look where all your thinking has gotten you,"
I want to tell him. And he can't even cry.
All afternoon I carry him around with me,
a weight that could drown.
What does he want? What do I want from him?
It's too easy to doubt the worth of everything,
to find the flaws and shortcomings
in everyone, including oneself.
It's enough to know they are there,
and then go on fishing,
down to the slashes the mill-boy glides.

FASTING DAY

For a while there I felt dizzy
and was almost looking forward
to toppling over. I figured,
what the hell, you're alone
in your own living room, how bad
can it be, you can afford a little
breakage. But then I stopped
and walked around steady as she goes
and felt bored. So I blindfolded
myself and started spinning.
As I was about to expire
from ecstasy, the phone rang.
I lowered myself to the ground
with great difficulty and commenced
crawling in all directions.
I picked up an old shoe, lost
for years, and said, "Hello. Yes,
I love you, too. No, I don't
want a new credit card. Must run,
something's boiling over."
My dislocation is unknown.
I am starting to coo
lachrymosely
like a gardenia
in a black mist,
o coo.

SCATTERED REFLECTIONS

I cabled my lawyer about the incident,
then returned to the hotel bar
and ordered a whiskey. The dame
sitting next to me was tight
but not as tight as her sweater.
Later, I helped her catch a taxi
and gave her some money for the ride home.
God knows I like the ladies but
I like to think I'm a gentleman
and wouldn't take advantage of one
when she's down on her luck.
I've been down too often myself.
And only myself to blame—love,
booze, stupidity, mix 'em up
and you find yourself babbling
to God in Arabic about a demonic cat
living in your head next to the
fiery urinal. I've been there
and back more times than I care
to remember. When I was young
I thought respectable meant dead.
I liked the dark side of life,
the hoods, fast girls, and nights
that told a thousand stories.
And then at some invisible point
you realize it is the same story
told over and over, and that's
when you either move on or die.
I went out west and worked on a ranch
for a couple of years, learned to ride,
brand, you name it. I was a cowboy
and loved every minute of it.
I missed the women, but there was
no time for that, so I visited them

in my dreams. I'd fall in bed after dinner
and pick an old favorite and call
her up, dancing, kissing, all of it.
We never fought, had no problems.
Sometimes in the morning I would be
surprised to find myself alone in bed.
As I said, I liked the work, but I
also know that this was not my real life.
I had no idea what my real life was,
but I knew I had to look for it.
So one day I packed my car and took off.
I drove the whole country, examining
homes, stores, businesses, streets,
people, like a crazed inspector general,
when all I was looking for was me.
I concluded that there was no me,
just flutterings, shudderings and shadows.
I think most people feel the same way,
and it isn't bad, floating under the stars
at night like fireflies sending signals.

NO EXPLANATION

Down the street they are pulverizing the old
police station. They started by crushing it,
then they beat it, and then they proceeded to
grind it up. I walked by it just a few minutes
ago. All that's left is a mountain of woodchips. . . .
"Where are the policemen?" I asked one of the
workers. He pointed to the mountain of woodchips
and said, "We never saw them." I walked on
thinking about Officer Plotkin, how he'd arrested
me when I was guilty, and how he'd come to my aid
when I'd needed him. I stopped and looked back
over my shoulder. I longed to be arrested,
to be saved.

THE LONDON TIMES

We had walked several hours from our hotel
to find Queen Mary's Garden. Roses were in full
bloom as far as we could see, hundreds of varieties
of roses. The fragrances mingling in the air were
intoxicating. A pond reflected the roses along
its banks. All the variations of peach, pink,
red, yellow and white were inflaming our vision.
It is widely rumored that the current Queen pees
a little on each rose every morning.

THE END OF ZEN

There was a very tiny frog sitting on a fallen
leaf staring into space and hoping for an aphid to
fly by. A boy spotted it and picked it up and took
it into his house to show his mother and sister.
They loved it and made a little home for it in an
insect box. Nobody thought about the little frog's
family. Two days later they returned the frog to
the very same leaf upon which they had found it.
It was a day of solemn, good news. An hour or so
passed, and then a golden mayfly flew by. The frog
jumped and swallowed it.

GEESE AT NIGHT

I hear geese passing over high in the darkness.
They fly higher than any other bird. Their honking
sounds as if filtered through miles of fog. But
thanks to the harvest moon I can see them, just barely.
The V formation shifts to a checkmark, the checkmark
crumbles, and so on, always changing and reforming.
After they have disappeared, their honking still
floats back to me, an immortal celebration and a
brief farewell.

YOU THINK YOU KNOW A WOMAN

I am thinking of her almond breath
and her irrefutable impact on orthodox mathematics
and physics as well. She's also a spider,
of some sort, and a little bit of vanilla pudding.
Her soft curves, her beehives, her waterfalls
and deserts also cross my mind, as well as her
narcotics and magnolias, her sables and minks
and fumigations, as well as her oracles and demarcations.
How many comets has she actually seen?
I don't know. But I do know her favorite spots in
Delaware, and her mystery play, her radar, her shorthand.
Her gift as a topiarist and her dew point.
Her carrots and mangoes and chimney sweeps.
She saved a rock about to fall from a ledge.
She found some socks thrown into a corner.

CURIOUS

Gabriella was lying on her back naked
on the living room rug when an antique toy
airplane came buzzing out of the sky and landed
just below her breasts and taxied to the edge
of her pubis. I had been painting a wall but
immediately put down my brush. She was smiling.
    "That was an incredible landing," I said.
    "Perfect," she replied.
My arousal embarrassed me.
    "Just for you," she said, "I'll do it again."

DENIED AREAS

Some zones you have to walk around.
We have no idea what goes on inside them,
we just give them a wide berth and look
around for the friendlier zones. Sometimes
you have to take running leaps to get to
them. We keep moving, not always in straight
lines but we keep moving. And we can chat,
"How's the weather?" "I don't know."
"How's your mother?" "I don't have a
mother." It can be stressful, though
sometimes we break into song without
warning, and then someone always starts
to remember another life, and then one by
one we all begin to weep and anything
seems possible like a glistening rainy
pavement, or a lodging house, a toothpick.

NIGHT BLINDNESS

There was a charming party at the Caskeys'.
Everyone was drinking rum punch out of those
crystal cups. Waiters in cutaway morning coats
offered an endless variety of delicacies. Cheer-
ful music played throughout the evening. Many
women displayed their bosoms tastefully. Men
tried not to notice, but that seemed a bit rude,
so they would smile into the cleavage and nearly
lose their balance in admiration. Alvin Novak
got his nose stuck in Hilda Hauser's and had to
be helped out. Hilda brashly said to the morti-
fied Alvin, "Did you find anything you liked in
there?" To which Alvin replied, "There's something
satisfying about doing a little manual labor."

TO BEG FOR FOOD IN A CONTEMPTIBLE WAY

You have to imagine that your pain
has become something else, a pet of some
kind, a little doggy, and that it follows
you everywhere you go because it loves you
and wants to protect you. It is there when
you get up in the morning, it goes to the
office with you, it goes shopping with you,
it even goes to the movies with you. It is
the most loyal pet you have ever had. Then
one day when you are fed up with it, with
its chuckleheaded constancy, you drive it
out to the countryside and dump it by the
side of the road. When you get back home
there is no doggy, there is just the pain,
and that is somewhat of a relief in itself.

THE SHIFTING DAPPLES OF SUNLIGHT

Julie was painting my portrait. I
had been sitting for her for two weeks.
We barely talked, and of course I tried
not to move. My neck ached, my back was
killing me. At the end of each day we
drank scotch and laughed and sometimes
rolled around on the floor. That was
about the only exercise I got. My
impatience was killing me. All during
the sitting my own thoughts swarmed my
brain with a turbulence that was downright nauseating, surfing through the
rough waters of time without a map.
When the painting was finally finished
I shuddered to imagine what grotesque
creature she might have captured—
old pipes obstructed by sludge, the
dreams of Russian peasant women and
utter sloth, a swimmer's pale yellow
teeth. But, alas, there was none of
that. There was just me, looking happy
with my hair thinning and my big blue
eyes saying whoopee I'm alive.

TORTURE

Eleanor goes to see her psychiatrist
twice a week. Whatever she tells him he
invariably tells her that it is normal to feel
that way. She tells him that she wants to
kill herself and he says everybody does.
She tells him she wants to make love in
a crowded restaurant and he says of course
that is a perfectly normal thing to want.
She tells him most days she can't get out
of bed and she can't stop crying for hours
at a time. He says that's the basic human
condition. Before her decline into this
maelstrom she was a loving, caring person
with many friends and interests. Now it
seems the doctor has convinced her that
everyone is just like her so why bother,
they're jerks, and she alone stars in the
drama of the century: ELEANOR, Ruthless
Conqueror of the Dark Ages.

HER SILHOUETTE AGAINST
THE ALPENGLOW

Climbing a mountain is very hard work,
so we just sat at the bottom of it and ate
our picnic. Others came along and actually
started to climb it. They were tough and
strong but we still thought they were foolish, but refrained from telling them so.
They were loaded down with so much equipment
they could barely walk on level ground—ropes,
sleeping bags, ice axes, oxygen masks—
whereas for a picnic you can get everything
you need into a basket—wine, cheese, salami,
bread, napkins. "Marie," I say, "Do you
still love me?" "Chuck you, Farley," she
says, "and your whole famn damily. You know
I'll always love you. All hotsie-dandy here,
thank you very much."

HANGING BY A THREAD

It was almost midnight, but the full moon
lit up the newly fallen snow and even the trees
were glittering. The children were wakened by
the light and wanted to go sledding. It all
seemed so magical we couldn't say no. With a
fire blazing in the fireplace, Anne and I watched
from the living room window as Sophie, Ben and
Peter raced down the hill looking as happy as
children can be, squealing and tumbling into
the great drifts. Over and over they would climb
back up the hill and repeat the whole spectacle.
Eventually, Anne and I fell asleep on the couch
under a warm wool quilt. When we woke in the
early morning the first thing we did was check
on the kids. Each was sound asleep in their
bed. At breakfast we asked them how late they
had stayed out. They looked puzzled, what did
we mean? They had gone to bed early and slept
well. They knew nothing about sledding at
midnight, nothing at all. "Perhaps later today
we'll all go sledding," I said. "I have too
much homework," Sophie said. Ben and Peter
agreed.

CHIRPY, THE RUFFIAN

We were on our way out to the beach
to visit some whales we had gotten to know
slightly when the car suddenly exploded.
Mercifully, we were spared, or some of us
were spared anyway. Bodo looked as sharp
as ever, like a smoky Egyptian cat eager
to be fed. Perhaps some terrorist had
gotten to us, God knows we have made our
fair share of enemies! We were the Sand People,
we ate sand. The wind blew right through
us and we kept walking, kept falling down.

SNAKE CHARMING SECRETS OF THE INDIAN SUBCONTINENT

I was seated at the bar having my usual
five o'clock cocktail, a martini. It had been
a hellish day at the office and I was trying to
shake off some of the tension. "Can I have your
olive?" the stranger sitting next to me asked.
"Hell, no," I answered testily. "Well, then, can
I have a sip, I've never tasted a martini."
"Get your own," I said. That shut him up. I
went back to my thoughts. The boss was driving
me too hard, maybe looking for an excuse to
let me go. I wouldn't be the first. I stared
into the mirror behind the bar. The man next
to me looked truly wretched. "What's your
problem, pal?" I said to him. "You're not
eating your olive," he said.

DOINK

I am a scientist who don't know nothing
yet. But every morning I peer into my micro-
scope to see if any wee thing be swimming
around. (Once I thought I saw a dog of some
kind.) And every night I look through my
telescope to see if anything's fluttering or
sputtering in the sky (I've spotted several
stars and named them all after me, Prince
Hubertus zu Lowenstein). In the afternoons
I read ladies' fashion magazines. They sharpen
my mind and give me many of my best ideas.
When my wife, the Princess, sees me in my
latest outfit she always says, "Cowabunga!"
several times.

SOMEHOW NOT AWARE THAT SHE WAS
HEAVEN-BORN

The sun was shining through the rain
thus creating the effect of a second coming
not of Christ but of some eerie one-eyed
beast, bodiless save for the eye, which in
itself is bleary and sad. A thunderclap
scared me half to death. I was just sitting
in my chair growing a beard, my brain lit up
like a pinball machine and I prayed for order.
Yolanda asked me if I wanted a sandwich.
"A sandwich is perhaps our only hope, our
best hope, our last chance to survive this
big blow. You are a saint and a genius,
Yolanda," I said. "Get it yourself," she
said.

FROM THE MORNING TWILIGHT TO
THE GLOAMING

In church last Sunday the minister shocked
the whole congregation by telling us that we were
all lazy and selfish and venal and that we were
all hypocrites and didn't give a damn about the
poor. He was shaking he was so mad. He said
we didn't deserve the Lord's love and forgive-
ness. He said we could rot in hell for all he
cared. That's when I threw my hymnal at him.
Many of the women were sobbing rather loudly,
but I could see plenty of the men had had more
than their full and were ready to do something
about it. A bloodthirsty lynch mob was forming
in the aisles. I know these men, they're good
citizens, good fathers and husbands, who take
their religion seriously, but if you mess with
them they'll kill you. The minister, seeing
the fire in their eyes, broke out laughing and
assured the congregation that he'd just been
kidding them, having a little fun with us.
A little nervous laughter started to build and
it broke loose into a collective roar that
couldn't be stopped. We all agreed later that
it was the best sermon he had ever given and
we loved him more than ever.

A CHILDREN'S STORY ABOUT AN ANEMIC BEDBUG

The man sitting next to me on the airplane
said he was an international arms dealer. He also
said that he had written poetry in his youth and
that it had made him very happy and that he wasn't
quite sure why he had quit it and how he had ended
up doing what he does now. I got the impression
that he dealt with some pretty unsavory characters,
dictators, terrorists, the bottom scum of humanity.
He was obviously very wealthy, but lived with a
certain degree of fear and dread. I offered him
a mint and he scrutinized it as if it might be laced
with belladonna. He looked me straight in the eyes
and then with a certain amount of shame took it
and thanked me. I put the mints back into my
breast pocket without taking one myself. That's
when he took out his handkerchief and spit the mint
discreetly into it. We sat there in silence for a
long time, slowly turning to ash on a windswept
wilderness.

TO EACH HIS OWN

When Joey returned from the war he worked
on his motorcycle in the garage most days. A
few of his old buddies were still around—Bobby
and Scooter—and once or twice a week they'd
go down to the club and have a few beers. But
Joey never talked about the war. He had a
tattoo on his right hand that said DEVI and he
wouldn't even tell what that meant. Months
passed and Joey showed no interest in getting
a job. His old Indian motorcycle ran like a
top, it gleamed, it purred. One night at dinner
he shocked us all by saying, "Devi's coming to
live with us. It's going to be difficult. She's
an elephant."

BURNT GREEN EARTH

He was a bold little tyke even at the age
of three. He would have fought bulls if given
half a chance. He would have robbed trains.
He would have rescued women from waterfalls.
He ate like a full-grown glutton, and when he
was finished all the walls and floors of the
house were covered with food he'd flung for the
joy of it. He was so fast on his feet his mother
and father could never catch him. He found
everything immensely funny, even falling down
staircases. He was always proud of his wounds.
His parents seemed exhausted all the time. They
looked terrible. When they finally fell asleep
at night the child would climb out of his bed
and work on his novel about the frailty of the
human race and the unwhisperable starry night sky.

ALL OVER THE LOT

We were at the ballgame when a small child
came up to me and thwacked me in my private area.
He turned and walked away without a single word.
I was in horrible pain for a couple of minutes,
then I went looking for the rascal. When I
found him he was holding his mother's hand and
looking like the picture of innocence. "Is that
your son?" I asked of the lady. She shot me a
look that could fry eggs, and then she slapped
me really hard. "Mind your own business," she
screaked. The boy grinned up at me. My old
tweed vest was infested with fleas. I started
walking backward. People were shoving me this
way and that. To each I replied, "God, I love
this game, I love this game."

WATCHING AN OWL SLOWLY WINK

Uncle Garland was a stern old man.
He was a banker and wore his three-piece
suit seven days a week. When his children
were grown he told them not to bother him
anymore. He put up with their foolish ways
all through their childhoods and that was
enough. The eldest boy became a champion
race car driver and died in a spectacular
pileup on live TV. Aunt Mildred went
berserk when they announced his death.
She grabbed a broom and began beating
Garland. He didn't even try to protect
himself. She didn't stop until he was
black and blue and bleeding all over.
She collapsed on the floor next to him
and for the next thirty years they never
spoke to one another again. No one was
allowed to speak their names in our house.

OVERWORKED AND HAUNTED

At the zenith of his acting career
Robert was still a nobody. It's just that
his desire to act was so great one treated
him with real delicacy the way one treats
the truly great. He strutted and preened
and dressed like a dandy. If he had any work
at all, say, a one-line role in a third-rate
play in an even worse theater, he would
isolate himself and meditate all day, and
after the play at the local bar he would
autograph paper napkins for baffled strangers.
One big drunk punched him out for no more
than that. And after that, Robert's acting
career, such as it was, began to unravel. His
pluckish spirit never entirely abandoned him,
and now he is a doctor in charge of neuro-
surgery at a very important hospital.

MORBIDLY ANXIOUS

A ladybug was walking along thinking happy
thoughts—he was very proud of his five spots—
when suddenly he looked around and realized he
was walking in a forest of dead ladybugs. A
junkyard of deceased kinfolk, many overturned
on their backs looking toward heaven. Thoughts
of his own mortality shivered through his wings.
But I was just a child yesterday, he thought.
Then he took off flying wildly around the room
singing "My spots are prettier than your spots."
He flew crazy eights until he had forgotten all
his worries and then fell to the floor and landed
on his back.

FORK-TONGUED

Half the people in town passionately
want a new parking garage to be built in the
center of town, and the other half just as
passionately do not want a new parking garage.
They have argued over this issue for three
long years now. It is front-page news in
the local paper every week. The two sides
are no longer speaking to one another. The
luxurious silence is punctuated by gunfire,
but even so it beats their petty words. The
mountain lion, thought to be extinct here
for more than one hundred years, is seen
downtown on every street corner, yawning or
scratching its ears.

NEGATIVE EMPLOYEE SITUATION

The Huntingtons had a live-in maid
by the name of Mary. Mary was very religious
and prayed a good deal of the time. In fact,
as the years went by Mary pretty much ceased
working altogether and prayed all of the time.
Mrs. Huntington cooked for her and cleaned her
room as well as the rest of the house. Mr.
Huntington would never rebuke Mary because
he believed her prayers benefited the whole
household. The Huntingtons were not themselves
religious, but they were superstitious. And
when Mary died after a short illness, they hired
another Mary, but this one cleaned and scrubbed
and vacuumed and dusted and polished and cooked.
The Huntingtons were terrified for their lives
and discussed plans for killing the new Mary.

THE RUG

We were more than satisfied with the new
Afghan prayer rug we had recently purchased.
It was very old and it contained asymmetrical
patterns that we could stare at for hours. My
head would start to swim and I had visions of
whirling dervishes spinning to the mad tempo
of the ragas until my head would nearly explode
and I would have to crawl out of the room to
keep from passing out. After collecting
myself, I would return to the room and resume
gazing at the rug. And this time a serenity
comes over me such as I have never known. I
rock in my chair humming a tune from the ocean's
floor. My lover is mother-of-pearl. Kali,
a rudderless boat is not so bad.

JUST TO FEEL HUMAN

A single apple grew on our tree, which
was some kind of miracle because it was a
pear tree. We walked around it scratching
our heads. "You want to eat it?" I asked
my wife. "I'd die first," she replied. We
went back into the house. I stood by the
kitchen window and stared at it. I thought
of Adam and Eve, but I didn't believe in Adam
and Eve. My wife said, "If you don't stop
staring at that stupid apple I'm going to go
out there and eat it." "So go," I said, "but
take your clothes off first, go naked." She
looked at me as if I were insane, and then
she started to undress, and so did I.

WONDROUS OBJECT

The company fired Willie just because he
insisted on carrying that little bundle of straw
on his back. It wasn't long before he was evicted
from his apartment. He slept in the park and used
the bundle of straw for a pillow. People liked
Willie and gave him food or money for food. It
was the bundle of straw that interested them, made
them feel tender toward him. He never asked for
anything, they just wanted to give it to him.
People could see it in his eyes: He had found his
happiness in a bundle of straw. People were grateful
for the reminder of something they had lost years
ago, and they set off looking for it with a sudden
passion as if trying to rescue a loved one from
a great fire.

BEACON

After teaching my class I went down to
the duck pond and sat on the grass. I felt
stupid, like I was a big fake. My own words
swarmed around in my brain like a cloud of
pesky gnats. I wanted to spray them with
some kind of lethal repellent. Several ducks
swam up to me and I offered them the bread
from my sandwich. They looked so intelligent.
They looked perfect in their duckiness. When
they quacked it really meant quack. I like
that about them. The green-winged teal looked
me in the eye for a long time. And during that
time my mind cleared and I felt calm as if I
were flying over a scenic coastline of rocky
promontories and the occasional white light-
house, and that was all I needed to know or
would ever know.

THE LACK OF GOOD QUALITIES

Granny sat drinking a bourbon and branch water
by the picture window. It was early evening and she
had finished the dinner dishes and put them away and
now it was her time to do as she pleased. "All my
children are going to hell, and my grandchildren, too,"
she said to me, one of her children. She took a long
slug of her drink and sighed. One of her eyes was all
washed out, the result of some kind of dueling accident
in her youth. That and the three black hairs on her
chin which she refused to cut kept the grandchildren
at a certain distance. "Be a sweetheart and get me
another drink, would you, darling?" I make her a really
strong one. "I miss the War, I really do. But your
granddaddy was such a miserable little chickenshit he
managed to come back alive. Can you imagine that? And
him wearing all those medals, what a joke! And so I
had to kill him, I had no choice. I poisoned the son
of a bitch and got away with it. And so I ask you, who's
the real hero?" "You are, Granny," I said, knowing I was
going to hell if only to watch her turn to stone.

THE ARRIVAL

Aunt Birdie came zigzagging down the hill
on her old bicycle with her long-haired white
cat sitting in the basket looking about regally
as though this were a normal way to travel.
Attempting to brake at the foot of the hill
Aunt Birdie smashed into a spirea bush, which
sent Percy, the cat, flying. He landed quite
gracefully on the branch of a hemlock tree.
He looked down on his discombobulated owner with
supreme indifference. I helped her to her feet
but she was staggering badly and had sustained
numerous minor scratches. She arrives thus
for tea every Thursday at four. We can't convince
her to wear a helmet. "Unladylike," she says,
wiping the blood from her forehead. And Percy
doesn't seem to need one. "For sissies," he hisses.

THE CHOIRMASTER

Things were going swell. The monster
in the basement was sleeping more and more.
He was growing old. From time to time I
threw some raw meat down. I think he liked
me. It was like we were married or something,
we just lived in separate parts of the house
and never spoke. I know marriages like that
and some of them are pretty good. Oh, don't
get me wrong, he'd kill me in a second if he
could, and vice versa. Meanwhile, I have a
life to lead, and I do. I work, I go places,
I speak to people and they speak to me. Then
one night as I was reading the paper at home
there was a gentle knock on the basement door,
gentle but persistent. With considerable fear
in my heart I eventually went to the door and
began to unlock one lock after another. When
I finally opened the door my eyes fell upon
a very small man. He was dressed in a
dusty three piece gabardine suit and hadn't
a hair on his head. "Excuse me," he said,
"my name is Patrick Monkhouse, I seem to have
lost my way. I was looking for the Little
Church of the Valley. . . ." "You have found it,"
I said.

CLIMBING LIKE A MONKEY THROUGH
THE THICK BRANCHES

It was late at night and someone was singing
outside my living room window. I reached for the
hatchet under the cushion on my couch. It sounded
like "I Only Have Eyes for You," which was very
frightening, directly threatening my existence.
I turned all the lights off and tripped over the dog.
The hatchet got stuck in the floor and I had a hell
of a time wedging it loose, nearly lodging it in
my forehead. The voice went on singing, a lovely
voice of the female persuasion. A voice like my
mother's. I clutched the hatchet tighter and held
it over my head. In utter darkness I was slowly
dancing in circles and humming along with the tune.

PERFECTION

When Cecilia Smith moved to Lunenburg
she was immediately the most sought-after girl
in town. Boys waxed their cars, got new hair-
styles, read books—anything to impress her.
But Cecilia hated Lunenburg and thought the boys
were stupid and dull. She thought the girls were
even worse. And so she had no one. After a while
the boys got fed up with her disdain and forgot
about her. The girls did, too. The most beautiful,
the most exquisite girl in Lunenburg walked the
streets completely unnoticed. A shade, a wraith,
a shudder of whitish fabric, the dreamy breezes.

THE FINE RAIN

The poker game went on into the wee hours
of the morning. I lost everything I had and
then some. Don offered me a ride home but I
wanted to walk. There was a very fine rain
coming down, warm. It woke me up and rinsed
the sense of loss off me. I had lived my
whole life in this neighborhood. I knew everyone. Everyone dreams, but none escape, darting
glances, the lucky day to come.

INVISIBLE

A hermit is said to be living on the far
side of the lake, but no one has ever seen him.
They say he lives in a cave a little ways up
the mountain. They say he used to be a schoolteacher of some kind, and then one day he had
had enough. He's not a holy man or anything
like that, he just got tired of people's ways.
They call him Invisible Tom, though in truth
no one knows his name. He's just their last,
best hope, but I don't think he exists. These
same people, one minute they're digging furiously
in a corner of their backyard, the next minute
they're flat on their backs watching a television
program on marital impotence. I tell you, you
can't believe a word they say. And yet I've
seen the sunlight glint on a bronze flagon from
over there and I've wondered what that life would
be.

THE PLUMBER

When the plumber arrived to fix the water
heater he eyed me with considerable suspicion. I
told him how grateful I was that he had come
and he actually growled at me. I asked him if
I could get him something to drink and he said,
"I don't want your stinking water." I pointed
him to the basement door and he spat at me
saying, "What do you think I'm an idiot?" Then
I heard pounding and cursing from the basement
for the next forty-five minutes. I considered
calling the police, but knew they wouldn't
believe me. I considered getting in my car and
just getting the hell out of there. As he came
up the steps I could hear him whimpering, actually sobbing. He opened the door and threw his
arms around me. "I can't fix it!" he said. "I'm
a terrible plumber!" I held him in my arms and
we rocked back and forth with me gently patting
him on the back. A little while after he was
able to leave, his wife called to ask if he was
alright. I said that he was just fine and she
thanked me very sweetly.

DREAMS OF CAREFREE LIVING

First I let the cat in, then I turned on
the kitchen light. I looked around, everything
seemed normal. I walked into the living room,
turned on the light, sat down in my chair and
opened the evening paper. NOTHING HAPPENED
TODAY the headline read. I heard a creak in the
wall, I looked around. I heard another creak.
The house was shaking. It was also bombinating
and rasping. I was holding onto my chair as
tight as I could, but it was tipping me out of
it and finally I sprawled on my belly and tried
swimming to shore. My cat stood there with a
mouse in its mouth and it wanted me to say
something and so I said, "Good kitty."

A NEW LIFESTYLE

People in this town drink too much
coffee. They're jumpy all the time. You
see them drinking out of their big plastic
mugs while they're driving. They cut in
front of you, they steal your parking places.
Teenagers in the cemeteries knocking over
tombstones are slurping café au lait.
Recycling men hanging onto their trucks are
sipping espresso. Dogcatchers running down
the street with their nets are savoring
their cups of mocha java. The holdup man
entering a convenience store first pours
himself a nice warm cup of coffee. Down
the funeral parlor driveway a boy on a
skateboard is spilling his. They're so
serious about their coffee, it's all they
can think about, nothing else matters.
Everyone's wide awake but looks incredibly
tired.

BEAUTY PRIZES

I was out working in my garden when I
spied a most singular phenomenon: a parrot
in my mulberry tree. I called to it to come
to me and it flew right down and landed on
my extended arm. It was beautiful and seemed
to be quite calm and friendly. I asked it
its name. "Pascal," it replied. "That's a
lovely name," I said. "Thank you," it said.
"My name is Nick," I said. "Hello, Nick,"
it said. I was about to fall in love with
this bird when suddenly it took off and flew
to the top of my chimney. For the next half
an hour I pleaded with it to come down. The
bird never even looked at me. I went into
the house and cut up a fruit salad for it.
"Please, Pascal, please come down." Nothing
worked. I was more than a little irritated.
Was it something that I had said? I was
nibbling at the fruit salad and flapping my
arms and squawking. A tall, bony farmer in
overalls walked up my driveway and stared
at me. "That's just what happened to my wife,"
he said. "You better stop that kind of be-
havior while you still can. Pascal's too
pretty for this earth. That's why I had to
let him go. Too damned pretty."

ASHES OF ROSES

A glen is a secluded narrow valley. That
required some thought because I wasn't sure if I
was in one or not. A raven dove at me and I dove
back. The periodic table ripped through my mind.
I was beginning to like it there, the mushrooms,
the fog, the root beer, the mayonnaise, the lepre-
chauns. Once the suds of the root beer had washed
over you everything about the glen was tastier.
Even the brussels sprouts and the purple mountain's
silver cloud.

A LORGNETTE, A PARACHUTE

I had been rooting around in the basement
for hours. It was dark and damp down there and
God knows what manner of animals lived there. I
found a bagpipe, a toboggan, a roulette wheel,
a movie projector, a blender, a vacuum cleaner,
a candelabrum, a croquet set, a branding iron,
a Chinese dress, some dental equipment, several
lobster traps and a bazooka. We had lived in
this house for many years and I had never noticed
any of this stuff, not that I spent much time in
the basement admittedly. Still, it was eerie, as
though a separate life had been going on without
us. And perhaps a more interesting life, that's
what gets my goat. And I have a strong feeling
that this is just the tip of the iceberg.

HER FIRST NOVEL

When Connie finished her novel she came
over to my place to celebrate. I mixed up a
shaker full of Manhattans and we sat out on the
porch. "Here's to . . . What's the title?" I
asked. "Well, that's a problem. The title's
kind of awful. It's called THE KING OF SLOPS."
"Gosh," I said, "that is unfortunate. I think
you can probably do better than that." We took
a drink and reflected. "It's about a hospital
orderly." "Ouch," I said. "It doesn't sound
very promising, does it?" "Is there a love
angle?" I asked hopefully. "No," she replied,
"everybody hates him. He's a creep." "Then
why . . . ?" "I don't know. I got started and
I couldn't stop. I wanted to kill him off,
but I just couldn't. He's the loneliest guy
in the world." "It's beginning to sound pretty
good to me," I said. "How's it end? Upbeat,
I hope?" "That's another problem I'm afraid.
He tries to marry a corpse, and when the priest
finds out he throws him out the twelfth-story
window." Tears were streaming down Connie's
face. I was desperate to find anything com-
forting to say. "Well," I said, "you could
call it THE GOOD PRIEST." Connie smiles, and
the wake continued long into the night.

LIKE A MANTA RAY

I can swim the length of the public pool
underwater. I like to swim right along the
bottom with my eyes open, and sometimes I find
things—a barrette, some change, a ring, a gold
chain, some plastic spacemen, a comb, nothing
too extraordinary. But this one day I was
swimming along and I spotted a pearl, and then
another and so on until I had both hands full
of pearls, real pearls. When I surfaced I
heard this darkly tanned, obviously wealthy woman
screaming at the pool attendant, "Someone has
stolen my pearls!" I quickly put the pearls inside
the netting of my swimming suit and climbed out
of the pool. I walked quickly toward the
dressing room, but then one pearl, then two, then
a third slipped out from my trunks and bounced
across the poolside toward a three-year-old boy
who had been listening to the lady with amusement.
He put his finger over his lips and smiled at me.
I had no use for the pearls and didn't want them,
but somehow at that moment I didn't want her
to have them anymore.

THE MAN OF THE PEOPLE

My bones and a lonely ache. My bones
stretching across the valley in search of
one bite of anything. The wind blowing
through them wanting a sign. The sun blind
to them. The animals sniffing them and then
running for their lives. My bones looking
quite impressive on horseback.

TICKLE ME PINK

Coco was an excellent manicurist, but
she tells me so much gossip it makes my head
wobble. Her boyfriend Benny comes too soon.
Her sister Sophie is sleeping with a married
man twice her age and has been set up in an
apartment that you wouldn't believe. Her
mother is spending all her time with another
woman of questionable orientation. Her best
friend Rhonda is torn between three different
men and is falling to pieces as a result.
Her other friend June has been a vegetable
since Larry did what he did to her. She
stopped filing for a second. "How's your new
puppy? Cute as ever?" "Run over by a
recycling truck. Flat as a pancake," I said.
"Oh my God, I'm sorry, I'm so sorry," she said.
Now the ball was in my court and it felt good,
dirty, but good.

CREATURES

The kids were playing in the barn.
They'd trapped a rat and were poking it
with a rake and a broom. The rat was
racing back and forth, back and forth,
and occasionally standing up on its haunches.
They knew it was okay to kill the rat
because rats ate the grain. The rat
would stop and stare at them as if pleading
for mercy. Horton landed a good whack,
and the rat was dragging one of its hind
legs now. Then Theo clobbered him. He
was an easy target now. "Let's stop this,"
Horton said. "Rats have to be rats. They
didn't choose to be rats. This guy right
here might be the Mother Teresa of rats.
Or the Muhammad Ali of rats. Or the Franklin
Roosevelt of rats. And who are we? Little
nobodies with a rake and a broom." And
with that they left the barn and headed
down to the pond for a swim. One of the
ducks was quacking, quacking, quacking.
"Frank Sinatra," Theo said.

PILLOW FIGHTS WITH MYSELF

The plunging neckline of my pajamas
was arresting, even to me. With my hair
standing on end I resembled a splenetic
porcupine. Poof, poof, poof, I was win-
ning. Meanwhile my thoughts circled the
globe in search of a more worthy opponent,
perchance a king or a queen. Why are they
never available to Joes like me? A little
fun in the middle of the night, only this
time it's a fight unto death, but softly
and with a lover's tuwhoo and ululu.

EDISON'S LATER YEARS

Shortly after I fell I pulled myself up.
I looked around to see if anyone had noticed.
Some small schoolchildren were tittering nearby. I approached them and inquired, "What is
it that amuses you?" A little towheaded brat
replied, "We saw you stumble and fall, sir."
"I didn't fall. I was practicing my dive. I'm
a diver by profession. I dive for treasure
and in order to succeed one must practice."
They were trying not to snicker. I was trying
to ignore the pain in my knee. One of the boys
then said, "So what treasure have you found
lately?" I reached in my pocket and pulled
out my comb. "Just yesterday I recovered this
comb from the ocean floor. This is the comb
of Julius Caesar. It has been lost for more than
two thousand years. The Smithsonian Institute
is going to pay me ten million dollars for it."
The towheaded boy looked at me in wonder and
said, "Mister, there's nothing wrong with falling.
Everybody trips now and then."

THE REPRODUCTIVE SYSTEM

In the still of the night a cicada began
to serenade. It told a story within a story
within another story. A man, who was also a
cicada who was also a python and a polar bear,
commenced looking for a mate. His thoughts
were like crystals, clear and bright. He said
no to this and no to that, and he kept walking
through every sort of weather. He was lashed
by the storms and burnt by the sun. As despair
was about to capture his soul, he found her
under a rock sleeping in a distant domain.
The cicada fell silent for a moment, an effective
dramatic technique. The man carried the woman
through more storms and more waves of heat.
When she woke, she recognized him. She had
dreamt him up and now he was here. The real
journey had begun. The cicada flies to the moon
trailing its song: Eat those packaged foods that
are at least somewhat nutritional. . . .

THE HUNDRED-EYED SECURITY FORCES

No one knew who I was. I got a room
with a view of the one fountain in town.
To the right was a church of some kind with
a steeple. To the left was a bunch of shops,
a shoe shop, a hardware store, an ice-cream
joint. No one seemed to notice me. But I
took notes on them. I wrote down all the
conversations I overheard and described their
appearances. Occasionally I worried about
my sanity and I recorded my symptoms, my
bizarre thoughts. I fed the pigeons that
landed on my windowsill. They had convinced
me that I was a man much loved and respected
in another world. What I was doing in this one
no one knew. Not so! I'm feeding some
pigeons and looking around and taking notes.
I am the newly elected mayor of this town.

THE OLD CANDY, THE NEW CANDY

Candy was primping in front of the mirror
for what seemed like an hour. I said, "We're
going to be late. You look great." She said,
"My hair's all wrong. It looks like I have
mice living in it." I said, "It looks the
way it always looks." She said, "I know,
and only now did I realize mice are living
in it." I said, "Mice are nice, I like mice."
"Where are the scissors?" she said, "I'm going
to cut it all off." "NO," I said, "you can't
do that." She found the scissors and started
cutting. I was horrified, but I couldn't
stop her. She cut and cut and cut, beautiful
tresses falling on the bathroom floor. One
mouse narrowly escaped having its tail clipped,
two others didn't fare as well. I never mentioned any of this to Candy, who was too busy
shearing herself. I hid my tears, too.

PRIMEVAL

I was standing in my yard watching
a woodpecker drill a hole in one of my trees.
I admired its single-minded industry. Mrs.
Cooper from across the street came over and
without any provocation said to me, "I hear
your daughter has run off with a drug dealer."
"What a powerful beak," I said, "isn't it
beautiful?" "You mean you don't care?" she
said. "It's a pileated woodpecker. They're
the largest of all the woodpeckers." "You
should be ashamed of yourself." "Mrs. Cooper,
Richard is a pharmaceutical salesman, very
successful. He and Sue have been married
for over a year and they live in Poughkeepsie.
Now please, please let me enjoy this woodpecker.
He, for one, knows what he is about and I
so admire that." Mrs. Cooper gave me her
standard indignant look. "Well, if you ask me
she still ran off with a drug dealer, and
that's that." The bird knocked a few more
times, then suddenly shot back into the forest
looking ancient and majestic. I kissed Mrs.
Cooper on the mouth and ran back into the
house.

FAREWELL TO A FRIEND

Where are you going? How long are
you going to stay? Will there be good food?
Chefs are responsible for more deaths than
gangsters, did you know that? Will there be
amusements such as swimming, golf, horseback
riding, fishing, movies, hikes, tennis? Those
activities, taken together, have caused more
casualties in the past ten years than America
suffered in World War II. Do you expect good
weather? What if it's bad weather? What if
the other guests are churlish or even cruel?
What if you take ill? Is there a doctor
nearby? Is he a competent doctor? Snakes, are
there snakes, poisonous ones? Are there bears
and/or wolves? Has anyone been killed by them
lately? It must be a favorite hideout for
escaped convicts. Don't go out alone. Are
you taking enough weapons? Those old lodges
are never fireproof. And fire is the most
dreadful way to go. I myself shall remain
at home, though I am well aware that most
accidents occur in the home. Perhaps I should
come with you after all. I'd rather my obit-
uary read, "Eaten by wolves at eventide near
the Frank Church River of No Return."

THE BLACK DOG

It was about two o'clock in the morning
when the poker game broke up. Everyone was
tired or drunk or broke. We were standing
out on the lawn of Bob Blackburn's house
when this big black dog appeared out of no-
where and started barking and hissing at us.
It was a mean-looking thing and it lunged
at us as if it meant business. I'm not
usually afraid of dogs, but this one wanted
to take us all on. Bob suddenly ran into
his house and half a minute later returned
with his shotgun. He told us to step back
and we did. He took aim and fired at the
dog. The dog whimpered once and then
collapsed. "Jesus, Bob," I said. "That dog's
bit me three times before. But still,"
I said, "a biting dog is not as bad as a
killing man." No one spoke. It was a silence
that signaled the end of something, poker,
friendship, and something more. The unknown
was already welcoming me into its secret heart.

Anne was crawling around on the floor,
presumably looking for something. So I got
down on my knees and started crawling with
her. An hour went by like that, my knees
hurting like hell. I couldn't take it any
longer and said, "What are you looking for,
Anne?" "My life," she said, "I'm looking
for my goddamned life." "What's it look like?"
I said. "I don't know. If I knew what it
looked like I wouldn't be down on my knees
crawling around like this," she said. I
stood up and brushed off my pants. All these
years together, was that not a life, two
lives intertwined? I walked into the
kitchen and got myself a cookie. Cookie.
I take one into the living room and say,
"You see this cookie? It's your life, come
and get it." Anne stared at me. "My life
is a cookie?" she said. "Well, it's a start,"
I said. "An amoeba would be a start, a louse
would be even better," she said. "Okay,
Mrs. Louse, how is Mr. Louse? Causing misery
for some poor, innocent schoolchild I suspect."
"Yes, yes, he's very good at that. My heart
rejoices to think of it. But you know, Mr.
Whoever-you-think-you-are, you're pretty
cute yourself."

THE RAISING OF QUIBBLES

I studied philosophy in school and it
certainly didn't get me anywhere. It was
full of nitpicky tricks, semantic games,
abstractions that only an idiot would care
two cents about. "I think therefore I am."
Well, thank you very much, I needed that like
a hole in the head. Somebody got famous for
thinking that one up. Oh please, excuse me.
"I am drinking this glass of water therefore
I am." "I am not thinking right now therefore
I don't exist." Well, anyway, I didn't mean
to erupt like that. I'm completely out of
the philosophy business. I haul trash and I
I like it. People pay me to take away their
broken-down stuff and I usually fix it and
sell it. I exist pretty good, so does my
truck.

THE MUSE'S DARLING

The day started strangely, with a
hiccup. Then I drove a pencil into the
wall and hung my hat on it. This brought
me huge pleasure, a tingle ran up and down
my spine. I thought it was a mouse, and
perhaps it was, but I was never able to
capture it. I peeled, sliced and ate a
kiwi and that sent a bolt of lightning
through my brain. Then I saddled up my
horse and rode off into the dawning. I
arrived at work pale and exhausted. My
boss looked right through me as if I were
a wizard holding a glowing white wand.
I jumped back on my horse and headed for
home, determined to try again tomorrow.

PRAYING AT THE BUS STOP
IS FORBIDDEN

There was a riot in the center of town
last Friday night. Police arrested more than
two hundred people. After interviewing all
of them they could not determine what caused
the riot. Most of them were released the next
morning after posting bail. Several newspaper
reporters tried to question them as they filed
out of the station, but nobody seemed to know
what happened. I myself was there, but I
didn't know it was a riot. I thought we were
a parliament of owls patiently waiting for a
mouse to appear. At least that's what I thought
I was doing there, waiting for a mouse. There's
no law against that. These policemen are so
bored they'd arrest a beaver for building a dam.
The town's quiet rattles their delicate nerves.

DUEL TO THE DEATH

Mandy wore an eyepatch and walked with
a cane. Dressed all in black, she was really
quite chic. And she was intimidated by no one,
neither man nor woman. She blamed a hunting
accident for her blind eye and bad leg. It
had happened in Africa when she was quite young.
She was a great flirt, apparently incapable
of love. When drinking she could be very
bawdy. There was a group of us who had been
getting together, usually at her apartment,
for about ten years. It was a great group
of oddballs and quasi-intellectuals and self-
appointed artiste types. Then, without any
advanced notice to us, Mandy publishes her
memoirs. I read it in one night, and cried
at the end when she failed to mention any of
us even once.

I SURRENDER

A lady with a miniature dachshund on a
leash was looking in the window of a fashion-
able dress shop. I stopped to admire the dog.
She noticed me. "Its name is Bruno," she
said, "and it's two months old." "Very cute,"
I said. "You like the dog?" she asked. "Oh yes,"
I said. "Here," she said, "take it. It's
yours." I was startled, almost speechless.
"How could you . . . I mean, why . . . ?" "What good is
it? What can a dog like that do for you? I'll
tell you, nothing. It can trip you. It can
ruin your shoes." She handed me the leash.
"Take this stupid dog off my hands," she said.
"Well, if you insist," I said and started to
walk away. That's when she swung her handbag
around and bashed me upside the head and I nearly
fell to the sidewalk. "Do you think I would
ever, ever even for one second, consider
giving away my precious little Bruno, the
sweetest doggie in all the world? You'd have
to be a heartless monster to think that, you
idiot!" she shouted and whacked me again with
her purse. She grabbed the leash out of my
hands and strutted into the dress shop. I
stumbled through the mazy winding back alleys
of town searching for something, but what I
never knew.

THE NEW LOVE SLAVE

I watched the new neighbors move in,
a man and a woman and a little boy. I gave
them a week to settle in and then I went by
to welcome them to the neighborhood. I intro-
duced myself and offered them my services.
"Would you care for a drink?" the man said.
"Sure," I said, "a scotch would be terrific." The
woman, Joan, excused herself and disappeared
into the laundry room. "Let's sit on the
porch," Lee said. We settled into a couple
of wicker chairs. "If you ever try to touch
her I'll kill you," he said. "No problem,"
I said, "I'm a happily married man." "Yeah,
I've heard that one before. Just never forget
what I said. I don't want to catch you ever
eyeing her." "Lighten up," I said, "I told
you, I am a totally happily married man."
I finished my drink, thanked my new neighbor
and left the house as quickly as I could. Back in my
house, I thought, this old neighborhood is
in for some fun now. I studied Joan with
my binoculars. Lee's death, of course, will
have to look like an accident.

THE EGGS

It was a beautiful summer day, so Amy and
I pumped up our little rubber boat and drove
over to the pond. I was paddling us along
the shoreline when we spotted something really
strange in the water. There were these clusters
of large egg-shaped sponge-like things. And
we kept finding more and more of them. We
agreed that they might be from outer space,
that some kind of alien creatures might hatch.
Well, that was our joke, but we were seriously
haunted by these weird eggs. We paddled back
to the shore and went home, not talking. That
night when we went for a walk the sky was green
and it felt like the earth was shaking. "They've
hatched," I said. "I know," she said. "Maybe
one of them will help us fix our blender," I
said. "That's why I love you," she said, "you're
such an optimist."

WASTED

Dr. Barton just didn't like sick people.
He thought they were weak and stupid, or liars.
His idea of a good day at the office was to
give examinations to only healthy patients.
He thought people who had migraine headaches
were downright crazy. His patients often left
the office in tears, and he grew more and more
exasperated as the day wore on. By the time
he went home to dinner he was apoplectic.
"I'm going to poison them all one by one!" he
would bellow. And his wife, who was terrified
of him, would try to calm him down. "Now, dear,
I know you don't mean that. I think you're just
working too hard." One day Dr. Barton came home
early. He was pale and shaking. "Oh dear,
you look awful. What's the matter?" she said.
"It's nothing," he said, "I just need to lie
down for a little while," he said. And he did.
And never got out of bed again, and
would not let her call a doctor.

THE DROUGHT

We were in the middle of a drought. The
crops were stunted and the farmers were sad
and desperate. The temperature was in the 90s
every day, the ground was baked. George Fletcher,
who grows corn and whose crop was about lost,
brought in a rainmaker named Seth Abel Potter.
Three nights in a row he camped out in the field
and sang some kind of mumbo jumbo songs all night.
He didn't get paid if it didn't rain but he told
George he had the best damned track record of any
rainmaker in the country. When the third day passed
and it still hadn't rained he knocked on George's
side door. He had tears in his eyes when George
opened the door. "I'm afraid I let you down, Mr.
Fletcher, but when it does finally rain would you
tell your friends I was here and you might mention
my track record if you would." George looked out
at his runty corn and then he looked at Seth. A
man's got to make a living. "I will do that, Seth,
and thanks for trying. Good luck."

THE SPLENDID RAINBOW

The lightning woke us at about three A.M.
It sounded like a war was going on out there,
the drumrolls, the cannons exploding, the bomb
blasts, the blinding flashes. The electricity
was out. I found the flashlight and lit some
candles. The roof was leaking and the rain
was lashing the windows so savagely they rattled
in their casings. "What are our chances of
dying?" Denny asked. "Almost certain," I
said. We sat on the edge of the bed and held
onto one another. The lightning bolts were striking
all around us. "Denny," I said, "you are very,
very beautiful and I love you with all my
heart." "I'll take that to my watery grave,"
she said, "and smile through eternity." Then
we kissed and the sun came up and the rain
stopped and the birds started to sing, a bit
too loudly. But, what the hell, they were in
love, too.

MOB OF GOOD OLD BOYS

Why do people go to the theater and
laugh all the way through the really sad films?
This happens to me all the time and I hate
it because I like to cry through the really sad films
and it's hard to cry when somebody is laughing that loudly. Maybe they like to see
people suffer because they're animals and
it's not them. It makes me so mad I want
to punch them out. I mean, what's so funny
about a little boy dying or a dog getting
run over or even a hamster going up in
smoke or a mob killing Frankenstein's so-called monster, I
mean, that is really not one bit funny.
I even named my dog Frankenstein and I
cry every time I see him or think
of him. He is always trying to console me
but it never works. Life is as fragile
and as beautiful as a spiderweb and the
wind is blowing, always blowing.

A WALK WITH TWINKIE

Mr. Logan worked on the railroad for
forty-five years, but he had been retired
for as long as I had known him. I think he
was eighty-nine, and he had a Chihuahua
who was also very old. For the past couple of
years I had gotten into the habit of dropping
by after dinner to bring Mr. Logan a plate
of food and take Twinkie for a walk.
Twinkie wouldn't really walk, so I'd pick
him up and carry him up and down the block
and then tell Mr. Logan that we'd had a fine,
brisk walk, which seemed to give Mr. Logan
great, vicarious pleasure. They were quite
a pair. Each one staying alive so that the other
would not be left alone. The house,
which is dark and musty, is also radiant
with the flame of a great love affair—
Twinkie and Mr. Logan, my recumbent friends.

FRONTIER GUARDS

I'm surprised to find you here, I said.
Likewise, she said. I come here every night,
I said. I do, too, she replied. Well, I've never
seen you here, I said. And I've never
seen you either. How could that be? I said.
When we drink we become invisible, she suggested.
I thought it over. What would you like? I said.
Hold my hand and we'll disappear together.
Shazam, she said.

CARL'S SHOES

I was wading in the ocean when this pretty
pink bottle with a cork in it came bobbing toward
me. I reached out and snagged it. I held it up
to the light. There was a piece of paper in it
with some kind of writing on it. I walked back
to the shore and found a stick to help me work it
out of the bottle. The writing was very faded,
but I could read it. It said: "For a good laugh
call Carl 555-9407." I grabbed my things and
went back to the house and dialed the number.
An older woman answered the phone and I asked
for Carl. "Carl's dead," she said, "he died
five years ago." "Oh, I'm sorry," I said, and
then I explained to her about the note in the
bottle. "I'd like to see the handwriting," she
said, "if it wouldn't be too much trouble." She
lived in a small town about a hundred miles from
where I was, but for some odd reason I agreed
to drive over and show it to her that night.
When I arrived the house was filled with the
odor of pot roast and the table was set for two
and the candles were lit and music was playing.
"I really can't . . ." I started to say. "But you
must." And I did, and it was delicious. When
she talked about Carl it was almost as if he
were in the room. She adored him. After dinner
she brought in coffee and insisted that we sit
on the couch next to one another in order to
examine the handwriting of the note. It was
definitely not Carl's own handwriting, and it was
not his brother's. "Just some prankster,"
she concluded. "Oh, well, no harm done, and it
did bring you here, for which I'm grateful.

You will spend the night, won't you?" "I don't
see how . . ." "We'll have to share the same
bed, but I assure you it will be quite innocent.
I'm an old woman, as you can see. Please
stay."

HAYDEN AND MADGE

Hayden and Madge had both inherited
fortunes and consequently had never worked
a day in their lives. They lived in a huge
Tudor mansion and employed servants for every
possible task. Hayden had a workshop and
called himself an inventor. Most days he
would putter around in there until five when
it was time for cocktails. Madge was constantly
redecorating rooms and bickering with the
workers. By day's end they were exhausted.
"You mustn't work so hard, darling," Hayden
would say to her. Madge holding back tears
her hands shaking, "I distinctly told them
Aztec rouge for the drapes and they bring me
Aztec yellow, the idiots!" Hayden is thinking,
we forgot to have children, how could that
be? We were always too busy. We never even
talked about it. No heirs. We've built our
own mausoleum. Come to think of it, it's
always felt like a kind of an afterlife with
Madge, though perhaps I am the deadest of
the two. She at least wants it to look
right.

A TATTERED BIBLE STUFFED WITH MEMOS

I stood at the southwest window for
a long time just staring out at the field
and empty road. A hawk on the telephone
line studied the field for any sign of move-
ment, then eventually he swooped down and
had his snack. A tractor pulling a wagon-
load of hay has crept over the hill. Five teenagers in a green convertible passed him at
a great speed and disappeared behind a cloud
of dust. A storm was rolling in, I could
feel the barometer dropping. This is where
the chicken catches the ax.

A WINNER

A police car pulled me off to the side
of the road. I showed the officer my driver's
license and then he asked me what I did for a
living. I told him I was a schoolteacher.
"I have a few questions for you," he said.
"What year was the Rosetta stone found?" "The
Rosetta stone was found in 1799," I said. "And
what is a quetzal?" he asked me. "The quetzal
is the national bird of Guatemala. It is one
of the most beautiful birds in the world, and
was considered sacred by the Aztecs," I replied.
"Most helpful," he said. "And finally, can
you tell me the difference between a hare and
a rabbit?" "The hare has longer hind legs and
ears than the rabbit," I said. "I am very grateful to you, sir. You are the first driver I
have stopped today to give me correct answers
to all three questions. Permit me to give you
this gift certificate to Bart's Ice-Cream Shop."
"Why, thank you, Officer."

THE BOOKCLUB

Bobbie came home from her bookclub
completely drunk and disheveled. Three
buttons from her blouse were missing and
she had scratches down both cheeks. "Jesus,"
I said, "what the hell happened to you?"
"They all hated that book," she said, "you
know, that one that had me crying all last
week, about the girl's mother dying, and
then her baby getting sick and her husband
leaving her. They said it was corny, and
I just couldn't take it. I couldn't sit
there and make fun of that poor
woman." "So what happened?" I said. "Well,
Irene was laughing and that's when I got up
and slapped her. And she punched me in the
gut and I grabbed her hair and threw her to
the floor and kicked her in the face. And
then Rosie and Tina and that bitch Sonia
from Leverett all jumped on me and punched
me a hundred times and I didn't know what
was happening." "So when did you get drunk?"
I asked. "Oh, when it was all over we went
out to Lucky 7 together and laughed and
laughed about it." "A bunch of tough broads,"
I said. "Nah, they're all pussycats," she
said, looking badly in need of repair.

THE SHALLOTS

I was standing in the vegetable
department of the grocery store staring
at a bunch of shallots when a woman came
up to me and said, "You're in that television program with those two cute girls,
Paulette's Bedroom, that's what it's
called." "No, ma'am, I'm sorry, but I've never
been on television," I said. "Now don't
you lie to me, young man, I know what I'm
talking about. I see you every Thursday
night at eight o'clock." Another woman
walked up to me and said, "You're Joel Beesley."
I said, "My name is Tom Kelley and I'm a
housepainter." "Oh, you just think you're
too good for us, is that it, Mr. Television
Star?" "I'm sorry," I said, "excuse me,"
and I reached for the shallots. The first
lady grabbed my arm with a violence that
was alarming. "You're not going anywhere
until you sign this." She tore a check
out of her checkbook and shoved it at me.
I wrote my name on it and handed it back
to her. She looked at it, then wadded
it up and threw it on the floor. "I hope
Paulette slaps you silly next time you even
think of making a pass at her," she said.
"You're disgusting," the other one added
unnecessarily.

THE UNVEILING

Rory had not had a haircut in years.
She was a brunette with manes that cascaded.
In a slight wind she couldn't see because of
her own hair. She had a thousand gestures
for waving it from her face. When you were with
Rory it's all you could think about. In fact,
it's all she could think about. It was assumed
that she was quite attractive under all those
tresses, but no one really knew. One day she
asked her friend Marilyn to recommend a hair-
dresser to her. Marilyn was really delighted to suggest
her own, a man named Bruno. At her appointment
Rory asks Bruno to cut it all off, oh leave
maybe half an inch. Bruno at first refuses,
telling her she has the most beautiful hair he
has ever seen. But Rory insists. As he begins
Rory closes her eyes and keeps them closed
until he has finished. When she finally looks
in the mirror an hour later, she smiles, she
is very happy. When she leaves the shop she
feels that she is floating above the ground,
a free woman with clear thoughts. All those
years she has been in hiding, but from what?
Look, she thought, that must be a butterfly,
and there's a cloud. . . .

BITTERNESS

Halfway through the twenty-third
annual dog show someone phoned in a bomb
threat. The police were very orderly in
evacuating the stands, but the dog owners
were nearly out of their minds in panic
and the police were actually getting angry
at them for nearly causing chaos. The
owner of a shih tzu was screaming at the
top of her lungs before she fainted. A
woman cradling her Bedlington terrier kept
urging it to bite someone, anyone. Once
outside we were told to stay away from
the building while the bomb experts searched
it. Everyone knew there wasn't a bomb
in there, but still. Who would do such a thing
like this? Several of the dog owners seemed
to think they knew. They spoke in conspir-
atorial tones and promised a hideous revenge,
but not before a basset hound blithely peed
on their shoes. The world wobbled off its
axis and a foul wind blew.

A FRESH PERFORMANCE

A mishap on the set today. Julie was
to kiss Don on the lips, but she missed and
fell on her face. She broke her nose and
knocked out her two front teeth. I'm not
sure she's right for the part, but now it
would be cruel to remove her. When she fell
off the chair and broke her leg I was annoyed,
but I also felt sorry for her. Don really
despises her. She's always saying her lines
out of sequence. And she kisses as if her
mouth was filled with sand. Actually, I
think she's more attractive with her front
teeth missing and her nose bandaged up.
And the time she set the stage curtains on
fire when lighting her cigarette, that was
theater. The play will go on, but Don must
go. I'm tired of his complaints.

A LITTLE BIRDIE TOLD HER

Dodie came home from her yoga class
feeling as if she had just been in a car
wreck. The kitchen was a mess, but she
didn't care, she had no appetite. She
lay down and flicked on the TV. The local news
was on and a reporter was interviewing
a man who had just been in an eighteen-
car pileup on the freeway. "I feel great,
I really do. I've had a bad back for years
and I think this fixed it. It's a miracle."
Dodie switched off the TV in a fit of
resentment. Even her diet was backfiring.
All her efforts at self-improvement were
causing her pain. Her French lessons
increasingly muddled her ability to speak
English correctly. And she could barely
walk thanks to her yoga. Dodie began
nodding so as to appear wise.

THE REAL THING

Once I got my yodeling down good
I had it pretty much made. I traveled
the county fair circuit, but I also did
my share of weddings and bar mitzvahs and
school graduations and concerts of all sorts.
I'd drive my van and I'd sleep on a mattress
in the back and usually there would be food
at all these places. And the women, oh the
women are crazy about a yodeling man. And
I was making good money and stashing plenty
of it away. This went on for about five
years. Then one day after a concert, this
old farmer comes up to me and says, "Son, I
don't mean to be rude, but that's not yodeling
you're doing there, that's more like pig snorting.
This is yodeling," and he starts to yodel
and I'll be damned if it wasn't the most
beautiful yodeling I ever heard in my life.
And I've never yodeled for money again. I
bought me a small farm and when I'm out on
the tractor I yodel up a storm, and I think
I'm getting better and better as the years go
by. I'd like to thank that farmer if I ever
run into him again, but I imagine he's gone on
by now, taking his angelic yodel with him.

WE AIM TO PLEASE

I went to the cabin and said to
the pilot, "Excuse me, Captain, but it seems
as if I left my camera in the airport. Is
there a chance we could go back?" "No
problem," he said, and the plane began to
turn and descend at a tremendous speed. The
passengers were screaming and I was thrown off
my feet and struggling to stand. I crawled
back to the cabin and said, "Excuse me, Captain,
I found my camera after all. No need to return."
The captain said, "No problem." And the plane
began its turn and rapid ascent, and I was
thrown backward again, and the passengers
were screaming even more shrilly. But soon
we were back on course, and the rest of the
flight went smoothly, and the landing was
perfect. As we lined up to depart, the captain
stood at the cabin door shaking hands with
the passengers. When it was my turn he said,
"What kind of camera do you have?" I said,
"I don't have a camera." "You're my kind of
guy," he said. And then he hugged me. And
I kissed him on the cheek.

STILL THE SAME

Eleanor thinks she's in touch with
her departed mother. They talk twice a
day. Mainly her mother chides her for not
keeping a tidier house. Eleanor asks her
mother what it's like where she is and
her mother usually says things like, "Oh,
it's boring. There's nothing really to
say." Her mother usually tells Eleanor
what she is doing wrong in her life,
and Eleanor is still terrified of invoking
her ire. She criticizes the way she dresses,
the way she wears her hair, the men she
dates. Her mother never was a nice woman
and she is not one bit nicer now that she's
dead. I've told Eleanor that I would stop
talking to her if I were her. But Eleanor
says she feels sorry for her mother, to be
alone forever.

FOR ITS OWN SAKE

Harriet Bigelow sits on her hands and
tickles her fanny and this makes her laugh
hysterically. And this makes everybody else
laugh and whole evenings pass like that. There
are no conversations, and at the end of the
evening everyone thanks her and says what a
great time they had. They go home and question
their sanity and certainly Harriet's and then
they start laughing again and go to bed exhausted
and wake up refreshed. And when the next invitation
from Harriet arrives they are only too eager to
accept. I guess you could say Harriet is a
one-trick pony, but it sure works. It's a
tragic story, but that's what's so funny.

PENURY

Olive Wilmont was knocking on my door
again. She knocks on my door about once a
month always collecting money for some cause.
And I always give her something, though from
her expressions I can tell it is never enough.
"Yes, Mrs. Wilmont, what is it this time?"
"Do I detect a note of ill nature in your voice,
Mr. Stone? Because if I do—" "Oh, no, Mrs.
Wilmont, you are a model of the charitable
heart and your causes are worthy." "Well, Mr.
Stone, a bear had been getting into my trash-
can every morning and leaving trash all over
my backyard, and I complained about this to the
animal warden, and he said the town would charge
me a thousand dollars to kill the bear, what
with all the expense it would cost the town.
And so I am asking you to contribute to
my Kill the Bear campaign." It was clear to
me for the first time that Mrs. Wilmont never
gave any of the money she collected to charity,
but she had been living on it, and now she had
become so desperate since she had used up all
the obvious charities she had to resort to such
a preposterous one as the Kill the Bear campaign.
She was a heartbreaking figure standing there
with her coffee can held out.

WILD BEASTS

In the front all the weapons were
loaded. We sat there in the dark with
not so much as a whisper. We could hear
sounds outside—skirrs, rasps, the occasional
yap, ting. We were alert, perhaps too
alert. Ready to shoot a fly for just
being a fly. When you don't sleep you
start to hallucinate and that's not good.
One night this crazy notion started to
possess me: I said, "Who are our enemies
anyhow? We don't have any enemies. What
are we doing here? We should be with our
families doing what families do. I'm laying
down this gun and I'm leaving right now."
I knew there was a chance that one of them
might shoot me. Instead they all laid down
their guns and we walked right out into the moon-
lit night, frightened, now, only of ourselves.

HUNGRY HEARTS

Marissa was a good friend, but you couldn't
really trust her with secrets. Gossip was her
life's bread. I was sleeping with her best friend
Tanya, but Tanya hadn't yet broken up with Ivan,
who I happened to know, because Ivan is a close
friend of mine, was sleeping with Marissa. So
when Marissa called and wanted to see me I was
apprehensive. "What's new, Patrick? How is life
treating you?" she said upon arriving. "Everything's
great," I said. "I got a raise at work. I feel
good. I'm still running every day." "How's
your love life, Patrick? You know that's what always
interests me." Marissa was a bloodhound. "Sorry
to say, Marissa, I have nothing to report." "It's
very unattractive of you to lie to me, Patrick.
When I see you don't trust me, it makes me
very sad, like we're not real friends." "Okay,"
I said, "I'm sleeping with your mother. You can
see why I didn't want to tell you." "I knew it,"
she said, "Mother talks about you all the time.
She's obsessed with you. She can't even hide it."
"She's an animal," I said, "I just can't help myself." "Just don't break her heart," she said.
"Never," I said. As she said goodbye, I could
feel the red lights of jubilation flashing from
Marissa's hungry heart. I was happy to have made
her happy, and I knew her mother would be amused.

IN THE RING OR ON THE FIELD,
IGOR HUMMED

Although Stravinsky's fame rests entirely
on his musical compositions, he was also a for-
midable boxer with a lifetime record of one hundred
and three wins and only one loss, and that to the
brutal Harry S. Truman. But he also loved base-
ball and pitched in the minor leagues for some
years. His fastball was clocked at 105 mph and
he could throw a sinker that left the best batters
wondering if the ball had been sucked into the
earth by a demon. He composed *Pétrouchka* while
on the road with the Kansas City Blues, his team-
mates often helped out with difficult passages.
While drinking a couple of beers on the bus,
he'd hum out loud, and one of the players would
say, "No, Igor, like this, fortissimo."

DEMIGODDESS

Aunt Myrtle was very old now and lived
alone. We hadn't visited her in years. The
elegant mansion on a hill that I remembered
from my childhood was now in such shocking
disrepair it looked as if it might collapse
into a heap of rubble any minute. We opened
the gate and it fell right off its hinges.
The shutters on the windows were mostly gone,
as were more than half the shingles on the
roof. Aunt Myrtle herself was a mess, her
long stringy hair was filthy, and she walked
around in a ancient bathrobe looking like a
ghost. "This house needs some work, Aunt
Myrtle," I said. "It's the raccoons," she
explained. "They're out to get me, taking
the house apart board by board every night."
"But why would they do that?" I asked. "I
told you they want me, they worship me, I'm
their goddess, and they won't stop until
I come and live with them. There are hundreds
of them." "Hundreds? My God . . ." Naturally
I couldn't sleep that night. I tiptoed around
the creaky old house peering out of the windows.
Then around two A.M. I thought I heard something.
From the kitchen window I saw Aunt Myrtle
crouched in the backyard holding a plate of
food in one hand and stroking the back of a
standing raccoon with the other. They looked
like very good friends, indeed. And one is
enough in this world.

THE PAINTER OF THE NIGHT

Someone called in a report that she had
seen a man painting in the dark over by the
pond. A police car was dispatched to go in-
vestigate. The two officers with their big
flashlights walked all around the pond, but
found nothing suspicious. Hatcher was the
younger of the two, and he said to Johnson,
"What do you think he was painting?" Johnson
looked bemused and said, "The dark, stupid.
What else could he have been painting?" Hatcher,
a little hurt, said, "Frogs in the Dark, Lily
pads in the Dark, Pond in the Dark. Just as
many things exist in the dark as they do in
the light." Johnson paused, exasperated. Then
Hatcher added, "I'd like to see them. Hell,
I might even buy one. Maybe there's more out
there than we know. We are the police, after
all. We need to know."

THE WINE TALKS

Evelyn Rankin and I were having dinner
at Montecito's, the best and most expensive
restaurant in town, to celebrate the completion
of a big project at work. To help wash down
the fabulous foods we had ordered some very
fine wines. Finally, after hours of great
fun, I asked for the bill. The owner himself
came to our table. "You are a beautiful
couple," he said with a warm smile. "How
long have you been married?" "Twenty-five
years," I said. "We are celebrating our
anniversary tonight in your lovely restaurant,"
I said. "You seem so happy, so much in love
still. Please, let this evening be on me.
It brings me joy to serve such a happy couple."
"Oh, no, we couldn't," Evelyn protested.
"I insist," he said. "Thank you so much,"
I said, standing to shake his hand. I drove
Evelyn home in silence. I walked her to her
door. I had never even thought of kissing
her before. "We made him happy," I said.
"Is that so bad?" "Do you think we could have
lasted twenty-five years?" she asked. "Evelyn,"
I said, "it's been a perfectly lovely evening,
and now it's over." I leaned toward her and
kissed her lightly on the lips, turned and said
good night. For all I know she may have a
giant tattoo of Elvis on her back.

RIGHT CONDUCT

A boy and a girl were playing together
when they spotted a woodchuck and started
chasing it. The woodchuck's burrow was at
the edge of the forest and it safely disappeared into it, but the children did not
see this and kept running into the forest.
In no time at all they realized that they
were lost and they sat down and began to cry.
After a while, a man appeared and this frightened them all the more. They had been warned
a thousand times never to talk to strangers.
He assured them that he would not hurt them
and that, in fact, he would lead them back
to their home. They agreed to walk with him,
but when he tried to make conversation they
would not reply. "You act like you're prisoners
of war," he said. "Not much fun for me, but
I guess that's good. When I was a kid my
mother also told me never to talk to strangers.
But I did anyway, because that's how you learn
stuff. I always thought the stuff my ma and
pa tried to teach me was boring. But from
strangers you could learn the secret stuff,
like how to break into a locked door or how
to tame a wild stallion, stuff you could use
in life." It made sense what he was saying,
but the kids were sworn to silence, a brain-
washed silence in a shrunken world from which
they could already faintly hear their mother
scolding them.

TIME TO CONJURE UP THE GOOD SPIRIT

Howard had been a generous, kind and loyal
friend for many years, but then about a year and
a half ago he began acting different. He seemed
turned in on himself all the time, dispirited
and gloomy. One day he sold his motorcycle business. He called me and told me he was going to
take a trip around the world. He told me he was
going to find himself. I said, "Oh, come on, Howard.
At your age you know yourself perfectly well." He
said he was lost. And I said, "Good luck." He got
back a week ago and soon asked if we could get
together. In our favorite bar, I said, "So how
was the trip?" "I found myself," he said. "Good,"
I said. "No, Dean. It's not pretty." "What's
not pretty?" I asked. "I'm not pretty." "I've
always thought you were pretty cute, I don't know
if I would go so far as to call you pretty." "Dean,
listen to me. I found out who I really am. I'm
a coward. I lie. I'm not trustworthy. And I'm
terrified of love." "Well, I could have told you
all of that, Howard. You didn't have to go all the way
around the world to find that out. That's just who
you are. Now tell me the good stuff, tell me about
the babes, tell me about the adventures, the most
beautiful places in the world." Howard stared at
me for a moment, and then he started to talk, slowly
at first, and then faster and faster until finally
it was a blur of incredible images, larger-than-
life people, hilarious getaways in the night, Howard
on camels and elephants, Howard boxing sharks in
the nose, Howard, glorious Howard.

WORLDLING

Mr. Hewit walked home from the bank
every day. He bought a newspaper at the
tobacco shop and read it cover to cover
before making himself a simple dinner. He
had no television or phonograph. He had
never married, not by intention. He had
worked at the bank for thirty-five years
and was surprised one day when the manager
called him into his office and explained
to him—some explanation!—why it was important for him to take early retirement
at this time. Mr. Hewit, while hurt and
confused, reluctantly agreed. The first
week of his retirement was awful. He was
depressed and bored and listless. The second
week he started walking to town in the
morning—at exactly the same time he had
when he worked. He bought a morning paper
and started to walk back home, but then he
stopped and walked back to town, found a
nice bench in the square. He read the paper
slowly, then tossed it into the trash barrel.
He walked over to the corner by the pharmacy
and stood there. He watched the people
come and go, the young, the old, everyone.
He noticed the eccentricities of their dress,
their hair, their limps and pains, the lovers,
the toughs, the workers, the loafers (like
himself). His imagination was intoxicated
by the lives these people led, so rich, so
varied, and many, so painful. Mr. Hewit would
move from corner to corner all day, and then
at five he would walk back home. He had
found himself the best damned job in the world.

THE ETERNAL ONES OF THE DREAM

I was walking down this dirt road out
in the country. It was a sunny day in early
fall. I looked up and saw this donkey pulling
a cart coming toward me. There was no driver
nor anyone leading the donkey so far as I could
see. The donkey was just moping along. When
we met the donkey stopped and I scratched its
snout in greeting and it seemed grateful. It
seemed like a very lonely donkey, but what
donkey wouldn't feel alone on the road like that?
And then it occurred to me to see what, if anything,
was in the cart. There was only a black box,
or a coffin, about two feet long and a foot wide.
I started to lift the lid, but then I didn't,
I couldn't. I realized that this donkey was on
some woeful mission, who knows where, to the ends
of the earth, so I gave him an apple, scratched
his nose a last time and waved him on, little
man that I was.

BOOBIES OF FERNANDO PO

We stopped at a tag sale and there was
a blender that I was considering. The owner
walked up to me and I asked him if it worked.
"Sure, it works," he said. "If it works so
good how come you want to get rid of it?" I
asked him. He told me they had got a new one.
And I said, "Why would you get a new one if
this one still works?" "Upgrading," he said.
"So you think you're too good for this blender,
but it's just right for me, is that it?" I
said. "Listen, buddy, if you don't want the
blender it's fine by me, okay?" "So you don't
want my money, my money's not good enough for
you?" "Just take the blender and go," he said.
"So now you're giving me, a complete stranger,
a gift of this perfectly good blender?" I said.
My wife was tugging at my arm. "Come on, honey,"
she said, "this man's crazy, let's go." Back
in the car, I said, "I guess we showed him who's
boss." "You sure did," my wife said. "Even
free that blender was much too expensive." I
thought that over for a moment. "Didn't Nietzsche
say that?" I asked, swerving to miss a pig
in the road.

THE MAGIC FLIGHT

A horse broke out of the Saunders' pen.
It was a beautiful black gelding, not too large.
It made it to the highway and was galloping down
the center of it for all its might, cars swerving
all over the road, some screeching to a halt, others
narrowly missing one another. The police were called,
and three cars were sent, sirens blaring, lights
flashing, creating yet another hazard. It was chaos
out there, and the horse seemed tireless. The police
got out enough in front of the horse to set up a
roadblock, and the horse jumped right over the police
cars as if that were the most natural thing in the
world for a horse to do, and I suppose it is. They
called for more help and there was more chaos on the
road. It basically wasn't safe to be on that road
unless you were that horse. Now there were five
police cars chasing the horse. One truck had toppled
over and several cars had crashed into one another,
though no one was seriously hurt. As nightfall
approached they still hadn't caught the horse. It
seems it had left the highway, but no one had any
idea which way it had gone. When questioned by
reporters, the police spokesman said he wasn't sure if
it was a horse or just a case of mass hysteria.
The Saunders said they never had a horse like that
or, at least, if they did they didn't know it.

LINK

Lesley was going out with a man named
Link. "What kind of name is Link?" I asked.
"It's just a name, a man's name, I don't know.
It's what his mother named him," she said.
"What kind of mother would name her boy Link?"
I asked, rather rudely. "Listen, I don't know
a lot about him, okay? His name is Link and
he's very sexy and funny and kind," she said.
"Where's he from?" I asked. "I don't know,
maybe out west," she said. "Why out west?
You're just guessing that." I asked, "How
many times have you been out with him?" "I
don't know, I haven't been counting, maybe a
dozen times," she said. "What's his last
name? What does he do for a living?" I
persisted. "I'm sorry I told you about him.
For Christ's sake, he's the best thing to
happen to me in years, and you just want to
spoil it," she said. "Yes, I confess, I'm
jealous. A sexy man named Link, with no last
name and no past and no visible means of
support, why that's every woman's dream
come true," I said. "You know, Wendy, you
wouldn't recognize Link if he was sitting
right beside you on the bus. Whereas the
second I laid eyes on him I knew he was
Link and I knew we were destined for one
another and all the rest is just so much
dust blowing in the air, but I don't expect
you to understand." "God," I said, "you sound
like you're thirteen years old, Lesley."
"Well, I'm not. I'm fourteen."

WAR OF NERVES

Ziggy was playing with his toy soldiers
in his backyard. Some kind of big battle was
under way and men were being blown into the air.
Their deaths were accompanied by crying and
screaming. Red Watson was watching all of this
from his kitchen window. "The man's seventy-
four years old and look at him," he said to
his wife. "Maybe that's what keeps him so
young," she replied. "Young? He's senile, that's
all." "Why don't you go play with him, might
do you some good," she said. Red harrumphed
and walked away. Ziggy killed off another
squadron and let out a roar. He knew how he
irritated Red, that was the real war, and he
had won that one, too.

RED IN TOOTH AND CLAW

We were listening to music on the radio
when the program was interrupted by an announce-
ment concerning an escaped convict thought to
be in our area. He was armed and extremely
dangerous. We were told not to attempt to
capture him. His name was Mugsy Strickland and
he was wanted on thirteen counts of murder.
Then the music came back on, but I could see
that Helen was shaken. "He's probably all the
way up to Canada by now," I said. "I can't help
it," she said, "I have this feeling, you know,
that he's going to get us." "I'll go and load
my gun. Would that make you feel any better?"
"Oh, no, dear, you know my fear of guns. I feel
certain that he would find us then. Let's just
listen to music and try to have peaceful
thoughts." They sat there listening to the
music, certain of their own deaths, until there
was a knock at the door. A brown package-
delivery truck was in the driveway. Helen
opened the door and a man in a uniform handed
her a package. She took the package and said,
"Thank you, Mugsy." The man stared at her for
a moment. He saw the life leaking out of her
like air from a tire. Her hands were fluttering
and her eyes were blank. "You're welcome, Mrs.
Watson," he replied.

CARNIVOROUS SPONGES

At the church picnic I couldn't take my
eyes off Marion Chisholm's breasts. She had
really put them on display. Well, it wasn't
just her breasts. It was the way she carried
herself, always smiling. Her mouth, her eyes.
The minister seemed to be captivated by her.
He was flirting with her shamelessly. I went
over and broke into their conservation. She
was telling him about her flower gardens, but
it felt downright erotic. I could tell that
he was imagining her mouth all over him, and
her breasts were talking to him in a language
all their own, a soft but firm language, the
language of tropical butterflies. "My fire
bush is particularly lovely this year," I said,
"with its vivid orange-scarlet tubes." Marion
turned to me, batted her eyes and smiled. "I'd
like to see it sometime," she said. "By the
way, Jerry," the minister said, "how's the wife?"
Marion grabbed my hand and, walking away, said,
"I am Jerry's wife, you old goat."

THE GUILTY ONE

Jessie says he feels guilty just breathing
the air that someone more worthy might have
breathed. I offer him a sandwich and he says
no, think of the starving children in Africa.
And I say, "Jessie, this sandwich will spoil
long before it reaches Africa, and besides, I
don't have the postage, or even an address."
But he doesn't laugh. I don't know how he
stays alive he's so guilt ridden. If I suggest
we go someplace where there might be women,
he says, "Why would any woman in her right mind
want to talk with me?" "Because you're a nice-
looking guy," I say. He looks at his hands,
turns them over, then back again. "These are
the hands of a thief and a murderer," he says.
His absolute greed is beginning to show itself.
By refusing everything, he is having it twice.
Jessie alone is starving the planet.
His gluttony is making me ill.
"Jessie," I say, "go home and eat what's left
of Africa."

THE DIAGNOSIS

Lincoln was sixty years old when the
doctor told him he only had forty more years
to live. He didn't tell his wife, in whom
he confided everything, or any of his friends,
because this new revelation made him feel all
alone in a way he had never experienced before.
He and Rachel had been inseparable for as long
as he could remember and he thought that if she
knew the prognosis she would begin to feel alone,
too. But Rachel could see the change in him
and within a couple of days she figured out
what it meant. "You're dying," she said, "aren't
you?" "Yes, I'm dying," Lincoln said, "I only
have forty years." "I feel you drifting away
from me already," she said. "It's the drifting
that kills you," Lincoln whispered.

FROM WHENCE THEY CAME

There are these people in town who only
eat seaweed, and after a while they start
turning green and you can't make any sense
out of what they're saying, so I try to stay
away from them. They tend to cluster together
like jellyfish, which is good for them, I'm
sure. I don't think they believe in anything
in particular. They don't vote. They don't
care. It's just a seaweed thing. They probably
see things differently, I mean literally.
Theirs is a watery world. They float in and
out of consciousness, neither happy nor sad.
Pods of them floating downtown, seeking out
the seaweed source, the packs of carnivores
parting to let them through, not wanting to be
smudged by their brininess.

WHAT KADY DID

I was sitting alone in a dark corner
of Woody's Tavern drinking beer. I was
counting all the reasons I had to be depressed
and I had run out of fingers. Kady, the waitress,
came over and said, "Hey, Sonny, come with me
to the back room. I got something I want to
show you." Kady's good-looking, but she and
I always found something to be scuffling about.
"I can't, Kady. I'm too down to even walk
right now," I said. "This won't hurt you,"
she said. "Come on, I promise." So I got up
and followed her. She locked the door behind
us. "What do you think?" she asked. She
lifted her dress up and pulled down her panties
and showed me her ass, which had a beautiful
butterfly tattooed on it. "I just got it
this afternoon and I was dying to show it
to somebody." "It's really great," I said.
"That's it," she said. "I just wanted to show
it to you." We went back out to the bar and
I sat in my corner for the rest of the night
covered in glorious butterflies, of the rare
meat-eating variety.

SWIFT, SILENT AND DEADLY

Father doesn't like to talk about the war.
He sums up the three years of his absence by
saying, "The food was lousy." He has a drawer
full of medals and I know he was shot more than
once. Surely he killed, who knows how many. That's
what those medals are all about. Now he reads
the newspaper as if it were a battle plan and it
would be an act of treason to talk to anyone about
it. Battalion A moves here, battalion B moves
there. At dinner he eats to gain strength
for the night will be long, cold and dark. Mother
moves silently, with the certain knowledge that
she will die before this war has ended.

KINKY'S HEAD

"Would you like to have your head examined?"
I said to Kinky, who was holding his head. "Oh yes,"
he said, "I would like to know what's wrong with
me." Gloom was his life, despair was his only food.
I opened up his head. My God, it was dark in there,
and full of cobwebs with dead flies in them. "There
are no lights in here," I said. "It looks like you
have had no visitors in years. And there's not a
trace of an idea, just a rat gnawing on its tail
hoping to become a saint in some counterfeit hell."
"I love that rat," Kinky said. "He's the last of
my monsters, old skin and bones."

THE FLYING PETUNIAS

When I let the cat in I didn't see
that it had a mouse in its mouth. But then
it set the mouse down on the kitchen floor
and they proceeded to play cat and mouse.
How very apt, I thought. The mouse stood about
one foot from the cat and the cat would extend
one leg slowly and touch the mouse on its head.
The mouse would sort of bow in supplication.
Then the mouse would dash on and snuggle up
under the cat's belly. One time the mouse
ran up the cat's back and sat on the crook
of her neck, and the cat seemed calmly proud
to have it there. They kept me entertained
like this for about an hour, but then it
started to irritate me that they had this
all worked out so well and I threw the cat
out. The mouse ran under the kitchen sink.
I let kitty in when it was our bedtime.
She has her pillow and I have mine and we've
always slept very sweetly together. In the
middle of this night, however, I feel these
tiny feet creeping across my neck and onto
my chin. I open my eyes slowly and kitty
is staring at me from her pillow and I am
staring at her. Then I close my eyes and
she closes hers and we all three dream of
joining the circus.

THE MAILMAN

Our mailman, Leroy Fuller, was suspended
from his job recently. He was charged with
opening people's mail. He claimed that he was
protecting them from death threats. He admitted
that he had never actually intercepted one.
The prosecutor said that people need to receive
their death threats, they need to know if they
are in danger. Leroy admitted that he had never
thought about it like that. He was suspended
for one year. That's when he started writing
the death threats to all the houses on his old
route. "People need to receive their death
threats," he repeated to himself over and over.
"People need to receive their death threats."
Everyone knew the threats were from Leroy, and
they knew it was his way of protecting them.

LOVING NELL

I was smothering Nell with kisses when I
suddenly realized I was late for my lecture
across town. I was lecturing on Lamaism, a
subject I know nothing about. When I returned
a couple of hours later, Nell was still puckered.
We were going at it hot and heavy when Nell
remembered she had to meet a visiting dignitary
at the airport. During her absence I finished
writing an article on the history of dry cleaning,
but, on rereading it, found I had used the word
"breast" twenty-seven times. Nell opened the
door and I lunged at her and pinned her against
the wall, and that's when I realized that it
was my mother's birthday and I needed to go
shopping. Nell gave me a passionate send-off
and I promised a hasty return. I bought some
hopeless trifle and sped back to Nell's
embrace. I kissed her ten thousand times.
Finally, she pushed me away and said, "I'm
going to cancel my dental appointment." I
said, "Oh no, Nell, your teeth are precious."
As soon as Nell left, I checked my watch
and realized that the bowling championship
started in ten minutes. The Fiddler Crabs
will march to victory this time, I swear.

THE PHANTOM GARDENER

I was out weeding the flower garden
when a ray of sunlight bounced off something
on the ground and nearly blinded me. I
reached down and picked up a woman's diamond
wedding ring. A married woman has either been
weeding my garden for me or stealing my flowers,
most likely the former since it is the more
vigorous activity of the two. A married
woman is in love with me, but not wishing to
be unfaithful, expresses her love in this
benign way. Very interesting. I replaced
the ring where I had found it and returned
to my house quite satisfied, as if I had just
eaten a delicious pot roast supper.

SECOND GROWTH

"Humbly begging your pardon, sir, but do
you have any pills that would help me get taller?"
I asked the pharmacist. "But you are a middle-
aged man. No offense, I think your growing days
are over, at least in terms of height," he replied.
"It's just that I feel a second spurt coming on
and I thought a pill might help release it," I said.
"But you are quite tall as it is," he said. "No,"
I said, "I'm a very short man. I never was allowed
to achieve my full height. I was stunted early on.
My mother stunted me. And then my father came along
and stunted me further. It was a game they played.
And then they called me Peewee and laughed every
time they said it. And that's why I never reached
my full potential." The pharmacist had tears in
his eyes. "That's a very sad story," he said,
"but nonetheless you are a man of considerable
height. I'm sorry, I didn't catch your name."
"My name is Peewee, but you can call me The Stump."

LOOK AT ME

I was taking my morning bath when I
suddenly noticed a fox standing on its hind
legs peering in the window at me. It scared
me half to death, but then I saw how calm the
fox appeared to be, so I decided to just act
normal and let the fox enjoy me taking a bath.
I ran some more hot water and sank down in the
tub up to my neck and closed my eyes and dreamed
of a fox watching me take my bath. Later, when
I stepped from the tub and he was still there,
I realized I would make several fine feasts
for his whole family, so I dressed quickly
and ate some toast.

THE CLOSING, THE NOSE WIPING

The only movie house in town has closed.
We have to imagine our own now. Tonight, showing
in my head . . . oh, no, I hate that movie, that
movie frightens me, I don't want to watch that
movie. I'm watching *The Boy with Green Hair*
for the three thousandth time and there's no
popcorn and there's no way out. And I'm all
alone in this giant, old theater. A draft has
given me the chills.

HOW ANIMALS LIVE

Ted and Phyllis brought the monkey home.
It screeched incessantly without the slightest
provocation. I suppose it missed the jungle
with all of its fruits and excitement. Phyllis
said, "What if we let it out of its cage? Do
you think it would stop making that horrible
noise?" Ted looked around the house. "I think
it might break everything. It might even bite
us. You don't want to be bitten by that monkey.
You don't know where it's been," he said. Phyllis
was holding her ears, trying to block out the
maddening sound. "Let's just let it go, take it
out back and open the cage and run," she said
in desperation. "We paid a lot of money for
that monkey," Ted said. "Why did we do that?
Whatever were we thinking?" Phyllis asked.
"You said it would be good for our marriage,
remember?" Ted said. The monkey
at that moment succeeded in turning the cage
over and unlatching the door. He raced through
the living room breaking every lamp he passed.
He bit the panicked Phyllis on the ankle.
Phyllis fainted into Ted's arms. Seeing the
pain he had caused, the monkey became silent
for the first time. Ted carried Phyllis into
the bedroom and placed her on the bed. He stood
there and stared at her for a while. Then he
went back into the living room and paced the
floor. The monkey paced with him. Finally
Ted went to the closet and grabbed his hat and
coat. He picked up a framed photo of Phyllis
and himself taken on an Austrian ski slope
many years ago, then he put it down and left.
The monkey, not knowing what to do, looked
around and got back into his cage and locked the door.

THE SHADOWLIFE

They had been married fifty-five years
when Oscar died. Vera always said she should
have left him after the first month. Oscar
had to have his way in all matters, where they
lived, who they saw, vacations, dinners, everything. They argued every day of their marriage,
including their honeymoon, which was miserable.
Now he was gone at last and she was free. The
house was quiet, even if it was in a town she
hated. She was eighty-two years old. She
sat there thinking about all that she had missed,
a lifetime, really. She had carried on a sort
of shadowlife in her mind. The friends she would
have made were mostly dead now. She hired a
neighbor boy to collect all of Oscar's clothes
and tools and sundry gear and drop it off at a
local charity. She wanted no trace of him to
remain. It was so quiet in the house. At night
she sat on the porch and listened to crickets.
How do you start at eighty-two, how do you
explain? No one would understand, why should
they take pity? I will tell them all about my
shadowlife, how grand it's all been. And then
I will die and no doubt join Oscar in hell.
Perhaps death will have weakened him just a
little.

WHEN YOU ARE LOST

Ben and Andy had been friends since
high school. They were both married now
and doing well enough in their chosen fields.
They still liked going fishing and camping
together several times a year. This weekend
they were at Moose Lake. They had caught
several good-sized brown trout and were
eating them around a fire. Talk about
anything, or just be silent, didn't matter,
it couldn't be better. Ben said, "Jesus,
look at those stars, there must be a billion
of them out tonight." "Yeah how are we
going to sleep? It's like we're at some
celestial ballgame," Andy replied. "Who
cares about sleeping on a night like this
after the great day we've had?" Ben said.
"Makes a believer of you," Andy said.
"Well there's war and starvation, too,
but a night like this lets you forget.
And if you can let it into you heart and
truly keep it there . . ." Ben stopped,
afraid of his own melancholy. Andy
understood. He said, "How about those
Red Sox!" They both laughed, and bright
starlight from dead stars shone through
them as though they weren't even there.

SWIFTSURE BLUE

The Witherspoons invited themselves
to Thanksgiving. I don't think they liked
the food. They ate very little and never
mentioned it. Vernon verged on the surly
and Belle barely made a peep. The other
guests tried to engage them, but usually
they got one-word answers. Gene, the comedian,
got fed up with them and started doing
imitations of them right to their faces.
Both Vernon and Belle could see what he was
doing, but were helpless to do anything.
The rest of us tried not to laugh at first,
but then we couldn't control ourselves any
longer. I know it sounds rude, but they
deserved it. Vernon and Belle finally got
up and found their coats. Vernon came
back and stuck his head in the dining room
and said, "I've never been much of a wit
myself, but I appreciate it in others. This
was a beautiful Thanksgiving I know neither
one of us will ever forget." I thought he
was going to cry, and perhaps he did, too,
because he disappeared quickly and they
were gone. Gene was quiet the rest of the
evening, in fact we all were. Reality had
fled and was hiding down some rocky road
I feared to travel.

CAPITAL PUNISHMENT

No one was allowed to know the name of
the town executioner, and he wore a mask at
all times. If we spotted him doing his errands
in town, grocery shopping or whatever, we would
follow him and taunt him. "Hey, Mr. Executioner,
how many have you whacked today?" He's not allowed
to speak back to us, so we figure we really get
under his skin. We don't really dislike him,
it's just his job after all. We don't really know
who gives him his orders, some committee probably.
Mr. Executioner is married to Mrs. Executioner
and she too must wear a mask at all times, and
their children wear masks as well. They don't
even know who they are.

MEMOIR OF THE HAWK

I was sitting on a bench in the park when
I saw this large hawk circling overhead. I had
my eyes on it when it suddenly swooped down and
picked up this little baby right out of its
carriage and flew away with it. My heart almost
stopped beating. I ran over to the mother, who
was eyeing a dress in a window. "Ma'am," I
stuttered, "that bird just stole your baby. . . ."
She looked into the carriage and then up at the
sky. "Oh, I know that bird. She's a good bird.
She just took my baby to play with her babies
for a while. She'll bring him back in a short
time. My baby loves her babies. But thanks for
telling me. By the way, what do you think of
this dress? Is it right for me?" I thought of
her baby sailing through the sky in the claws
of that bird. "Well," I said, "I think the
mignonette green captures the amplitude of your
inner aviary." "What are you, some kind of loose
nutcase? Get out of here before I call the
police," she said.

RAPTURE

"If you sit here a long time and are real
quiet, you just might get to see one of those
blue antelope," I said to Cora. "I'd do anything to see a blue antelope," she said. "I'd
take off all my clothes and lie completely still
in the grass all day." "That's a good idea,"
I said, "taking off the clothes, I mean, it's
more natural." I'd met Cora in the library the
night before and had told her about the blue
antelope, so we'd made a date to try and see
them. We lay naked next to one another for hours.
It was a beautiful, sunny day with a breeze that
tickled. Finally, Cora whispered into my ear,
"My God, I see them. They're so delicate, so
graceful. They're like angels, cornflower
angels." I looked at Cora. She was disappearing.
She was becoming one of them.